Streetsmart Financial Basics
for Nonprofit Managers

NONPROFIT LAW, FINANCE, AND MANAGEMENT SERIES

Streetsmart Financial Basics for Nonprofit Managers

THOMAS A. McLAUGHLIN

John Wiley & Sons, Inc.

New York • Chichester • Brisbane • Toronto • Singapore

This text is printed on acid-free paper.

REQUIREMENTS:
An IBM® PC family computer or compatible computer
with 256K minimum memory, a 3.5" high-density floppy drive,
PC DOS, MS DOS, or DR DOS Version 2.0 or later, and a printer.

Copyright © 1995 by John Wiley & Sons, Inc.

IBM® is a registered trademark for International Business Machines Corp.
Lotus® is a registered trademark of Lotus Development Corporation
Quattro® is a registered trademark of Borland International, Inc.
Microsoft® Excel for Windows™ is a trademark of Microsoft Corporation.
WordPerfect® is a registered trademark of WordPerfect Corporation.
Microsoft® Word for Windows™ is a trademark of Microsoft Corporation.

Library of Congress Cataloging in Publication Data:

McLaughlin, Thomas A.
    Streetsmart financial basics for nonprofit managers / Thomas A.
McLaughlin.
      p.   cm. — (Nonprofit law, finance, and management series)
    Includes index.
    ISBN 0-471-04226-9. — ISBN 0-471-11457-X (pbk.)
    1. Nonprofit organizations—Finance. 2. Nonprofit organizations—
Accounting. I. Title. II. Series.
HG4027.65.M35 1995
658.15—dc20   94-37588

Printed in the United States of America

10 9 8 7 6 5 4 3 2 1

91445

Preface

What you *don't* need to know about nonprofit financial management would fill volumes—big volumes, with nice covers, intimidating titles, and many pages. These are the kinds of books you had to read in high school and college and maybe in graduate school.

This book is different. Most books in this field are aimed at *producers* of nonprofit financial information. At least, they make you feel as though you are learning to be a producer. But you are a *consumer* of nonprofit financial information, not an accountant, bookkeeper, or controller. You need to know how to be an intelligent user of financial information that *other* people produce.

People in nonprofit management rarely have any training in nonprofit financial managment. This may be because they tend to come from nonfinancial backgrounds, or because there are relatively few opportunities for this type of training. Nonprofit financial management is more than for-profit financial management renamed.

The financial pressures on nonprofit organizations of all types is rapidly increasing even as the demand for their services multiplies. In post-Cold War America, nonprofit organizations are increasingly visible. As a result, the pressures on managers, board members, and leaders of all kinds of nonprofit organizations have increased.

This is an exciting period for well-managed nonprofit organizations. The opportunities for furthering their missions, their values, and their programs have never been greater. But taking advantage of these opportunities requires the confidence that comes from specialized financial knowledge, and few people connected with nonprofits have the time to complete a full course of study. This book will fill the gap.

The purpose of this book is to concentrate into a single, unintimidating volume the essence of nonprofit financial management. The book has a deliberately practical focus. In my experience as a nonprofit manager, consultant, and college professor, I have found a universal hunger for practical, helpful information. Consequently, I try to present the things that have been most helpful to me as succinctly as possible.

I make liberal use of the IRS Form 990, the information return for organizations exempt from tax because (1) it is a standard form and (2) it is easily available. The IRS 990 is the only financial reporting form that virtually all nonprofit corporations in the United States must submit, so it is ideal for our purposes. When not using the form itself, I will often use a listing of accounts taken directly from it. I also key certain analyses to specific lines in the form so that you can readily apply these analyses to your own institution.

A 1988 federal law says that nonprofit public charities must be prepared to make a copy of the IRS 990 form available for inspection by anyone who asks for it. Some states also make copies from each of their nonprofit organizations available for public inspection. One of the inherent difficulties of discussing financial management in the nonprofit sector is that its tremendous diversity sometimes makes meaningful comparisons impossible. By using the only common financial reporting form, I hope to bridge the gaps between different types of nonprofit organizations so that the content will work for a broad audience.

When it comes to nonprofit financial management, the IRS 990 form is a sleeping giant slowly awakening. Its many potential uses are just beginning to be understood, and new applications are being devised every day. One college-based researcher, Bill Levis of Baruch College, has developed a model chart of accounts linked to the 990 that can be used by those in the field. He has generously allowed me to include it.

The book is organized in four distinct parts: analysis, accounting, operations, and control:

- Part One   Analysis

  What to look for from common information sources and how to use them.

- Part Two   Accounting

  A quick primer on nonprofit accounting for nonaccountants. A little bit of theory and a lot of practical guidance.
- Part Three   Operations

  Where to focus your attention and why. How to get the most out of your resources.
- Part Four   Control

  How to keep control while accomplishing your mission. What to do to be positioned for the future.
- Throughout the book, the symbol 💾 appears where the reader is referred to material on the disk discussed in the appendix.

This book is not intended to be a textbook. I have deliberately left out lengthy case presentations and complex mathematical exercises in the belief that you have neither the time nor the interest to pursue an elaborate course of study in the subject. I concentrate instead on the thinking that goes into sound financial decisions. Some of it will be comfortable material to many of you, some will be new. My intention is to present all of the information in a way that makes it most relevant to people active in this most important field of nonprofit service.

THOMAS A. MCLAUGHLIN

January 1995

Acknowledgments

Many people helped with this book in one way or another. I particularly want to thank Allwyn Baptist, Becky J. Cerio, Robert Cowden, Dennis Fusco, Jim Gambon, Robert Gardiner, Elizabeth Hart, John Joyce, Bill Levis, Marty McLaughlin, Wayne Moss, James Nesbitt, Mary Plant, Joanne Sunshower, Shari Sankner Sendecke, and Sherrell M. Smith. My editor at John Wiley & Sons, Marla Bobowick, provided much support, feedback, and guidance throughout the entire process.

Most important, I want to thank my wife Gail Sendecke and my children Paul and Emily. As always, their ability to share me with this project was my greatest support.

Contents

Chapter 3: Balance Sheets: How They Get That Way   **25**

PART ONE

Analysis

CHAPTER ONE

Organizational Structure: Programs and Corporations

The nonprofit industry is enormous. Nonprofit organizations in the United States spend over $340 billion each year. They employ nearly 7 percent of the total workforce and are responsible for 6 percent of the Gross Domestic Product. Universities, research centers, religious institutions, and museums produce priceless accomplishments. Nonprofit hospitals are major elements of our health care system and in many communities are the largest employer. Social service agencies provide a wide variety of services to those less fortunate citizens. Other nonprofits educate people of all ages and at all levels. Still others develop communities and support our social lives.

There are many ways to categorize this industry. The traditional way is by the service provided and, to a lesser extent, the size of the nonprofit organization. This approach may not be particularly useful from a financial management perspective since services and even size alone do not necessarily say much about the nature of the financial management challenge.

TYPES OF NONPROFIT ORGANIZATIONS

For financial purposes, a better way of looking at this industry is to sort it into categories according to the primary economic function the organizations perform. Six distinct types of nonprofit corporations can be defined:

1. Direct service providers
2. Information managers
3. Resource distributors
4. Support and development providers
5. Grant makers or funders
6. Social organizations.

Note that these groupings are chiefly for analytical purposes, and that the activities of many organizations can span several categories.

Direct Service Providers

These organizations are the classic nonprofits. Usually public charities, they are the hospitals, clinics, social service providers, and the like that provide some sort of direct and recognizable service to some or all of the public at large. Often major employers of professionals, these corporations provide a "hands on" service.

Financial issues in direct service providers vary according to size and funding source. One characteristic that many share is the need to assemble a workable mix of funders, and to be careful about managing the relationships between funders' requirements. Complexities abound in their financial management profile because governmental and quasi-governmental entities are often major funding sources. One study from Johns Hopkins University found that 29 percent of all U.S. nonprofits' funding comes from government sources. Due to the limitations of government funding, philanthropy must also often play a role in direct service providers' management, and the stakes are high if money is accounted for inaccurately.

Payment in this field is moving from the traditional reimbursement for costs incurred to a defined price for a defined service such as one finds in health maintenance organizations.

Information Managers

Another large category of nonprofits are the information managers—universities, museums, advocacy groups, trade associations, and a variety of similar organizations. Their role is to accumulate information of a predefined sort and share it with selected users, often in the role of broker. A university, for example, can be viewed as a broker between professors and students, or between researchers and consumers of research. Information management agencies range widely in size from the very smallest advocacy group to multibillion dollar universities with international branches.

Consumers of information management services are multiple and naturally quite independent of each other; their financial systems must be capable of handling unusually massive quantities of information. These types of organizations tend to have memberships; therefore, the financial systems must store information about the same people for retrieval and usage over a period of years. In effect, membership records are the financial data.

In practice this scenario dictates a financial system, especially the revenue tracking component, that is capable of handling large numbers of small or large transactions. Frequently, the financial task is paralleled by the program manager's need to communicate with hundreds or even thousands of people, members and non-members. Fast and effective data management often becomes the only thing distinguishing one information manager from another, laying a heavy burden on the administrative infrastructure of each organization.

Resource Distributors

Resource distribution agencies reached their zenith during the Great Society days of the 1960s. For a variety of political, psychological, and logistical reasons, the federal government did a lot of business directly with local nonprofit agencies, positioning them as the last stop before direct contact with eligible clients.

No doubt it was politically useful for these local players to wield ultimate distribution responsibility, thereby shielding the federal government from criticism. It was also smart to graft onto the organizations' existing formal or informal support systems rather than re-creating them from scratch. Community action programs from the 1960s such as antipoverty programs are a good example of resource distribution nonprofits. Heating assistance funds of the 1980s are a more current example.

The premiere financial demand of resource distribution non-profits is strict accountability. In many ways, they serve as the social equivalent of general contractors, assembling a team of benefits or service providers in order to accomplish a coordinated job. In other cases, they act mainly as a final distribution point for transfer payments, usually as part of an entitlement program. Their work typically involves outreach, evaluation, and servicing of eligible clients. From the funders' perspective, however, their real value comes after the client transaction has occurred and they make their reports to the payments' source.

Owing to the demand for accountability, resource distribution nonprofits' financial systems will tend to be shaped by individual transactions and the funding source's rules. Most programs of this sort are expected to track the flow of money, not the effectiveness of the programs. Accountability in this context means careful accounting, not managerial success. Perhaps not surprisingly given their role as intelligent conduits, many resource distribution nonprofits end up looking a lot like the governmental unit that funds them.

Support and Development Providers

The fourth category of nonprofit corporations refers to support and development groups. These organizations are limited in number but play a major role in areas of the health and social welfare sector. In size and focus they are not unlike resource distribution nonprofits, except that they concentrate on leveraging resources rather than simply marshalling them. Nonprofit assistance corporations like the Support Center of America are examples of this category.

Financial management for support and development groups will be unremarkable except when ownership or financing of capital projects is involved. The task in these cases often relates to properly valuing assets, estimating the percentage of a project completed, and properly accounting for and reporting on funds received. The difficult aspect of financial management in the property acquisition or rehabilitation environment is dealing with irregular flows of cash in and out of the corporation, and keeping track of what are expenses of the current period versus what expenses should be considered part of the capital project.

Grant Makers or Funders

One of the most common of all types of nonprofits, grant makers or funders can range from the very smallest fund-raising agencies to massive private foundations. Their task is to raise money and decide who should get it, and, in the case of private foundations, raising the money may consist chiefly of effectively managing a portfolio of equities.

One of the things that makes the funder's financial management job at least theoretically easier than many in the nonprofit field—foundation CFOs, block your ears—is that things like revenue management may have to be done by outsiders such as investment managers. No financial officer can be expected to have the skills to manage a major chunk of investments, nor would the responsible board expect it. Moreover, there are arguments for accountability that favor separating investment management from operational tasks.

On a broader level, to do the grant-making job correctly, the funder needs to operate in a planned, disciplined fashion. Happily, good financial management can thrive under the same conditions. In effect, a funder is engaged in the business of shaping and directing streams of money over a period of years. This is a profoundly different dynamic than most other nonprofit categories, and it should not be underestimated in the context of designing a financial management system.

For all practical purposes, funders are accountable to no one. While the technical aspects of fund-raising and grant-making must be handled properly, it is relatively easy to hire skilled staff to see to that. Beyond the minimal level of legal compliance in both the public charity and the private foundation worlds, no significant person or authority is in a position to routinely challenge the workings of a funder. Ironically, this can be as much a hindrance to good financial management as anything else, since there is the possibility that complacency will crowd out effectiveness.

Social Organizations

The final entry in the list of major nonprofit types is social clubs and organizations. Whether fraternities, lodges, sporting clubs, quilting associations or any of a vast array of other entities, they share the common theme that they exist in order to further the social interests of their members. Funding comes almost entirely from members' dues and from business transacted with members (such as restaurant and bar sales at clubs), and occasionally from rents or investments.

Typically, the financial stakes are low in a social club. Members usually have little interest in the details of financial management beyond seeing that the dues are collected and the bills paid on time. As a result, two of the greatest threats to a club's financial health are sloppy recordkeeping and fraud. The need for fiscal accountability is just as strong as in other categories, but much of the focus is likely to be on cash. One thing that tends to be true for social clubs is that their financial prowess is never any greater than what the membership demands.

STRUCTURE OF NONPROFIT ORGANIZATIONS

Programs

Programs are the most visible and best understood aspect of the nonprofit form of business organization, and its chief means of carrying out its mission. Also called services, projects, clinics, divisions, departments, floors, or any one of a thousand other names, programs are the activities of the nonprofit organization.

Coming up with a fair and workable definition of a program is difficult. Here's an attempt: A program is a coherently packaged group of activities, usually associated with a specific physical location, designed to accomplish a stated result.

Nonprofit organizations run all kinds of programs, and often more than one. Day care centers offer infant care programs, environmental groups operate recycling systems, museums run art appreciation courses, and so forth. The two keys to understanding programs are that they generally have some coherent internal structure, and that they appear as distinct choices to potential users.

In most nonprofit organizations, programs are like little businesses, with a structure reinforced by nonprofit accounting rules and one that has immense if largely unnoticed consequences for everything from compensation to organizational effectiveness.

They represent a delegation of responsibility from the chief executive officer, and so they are the engines of mission. It is at the program level where the organization's goals are accomplished or not, and therefore those in charge of programs carry heavy moral pressure to get the job done.

Notice the use of the word "moral" in the preceding sentence. Typically, the motivations of those who run nonprofit organizations are different from those who do the same thing in the for-profit world, and the motivations of program managers everywhere are often different still from their bosses. We'll explore some of those differing interests later. For the moment, we'll use the program as the smallest management unit of the nonprofit corporation.

Corporations

The next major level of nonprofit management is the corporation that "owns" or runs the programs. The corporation is a statutory entity established by the legally sanctioned actions of one or more individuals. As a legally approved entity separate from its constituent individuals, the corporation has its own continuing existence. In legal theory, corporations are treated as distinct entities just like individual people, and corporations have their own collection of responsibilities, liabilities, and powers.

Why a corporation? The answer is disarmingly simple: because it's easier for the rest of us. Corporations can be mentioned in the same legal breath as the individuals who use their services, work in them, or simply exist in the same state with them. All are on the same legal footing, in that respect. The complicated and narrower answer to the question has to do with such practical considerations as revenue source regulations and liability strategies.

Revenue source regulations and political realities often nudge nonprofits in the direction of a specific type of organizational structure. Programs such as battered women's shelters almost of necessity start out as single-service corporations, while older and more established social service and health care groups may have developed a multiple corporate structure.

There are also liability laws to consider when operating different types of businesses. Nonprofit public charities traditionally have been granted generous protection from state liability laws, although that tendency is beginning to change. It's a tradition

Types of Tax-Exempt Entities

Section of 1954 Code	Section of 1939 Code	Annual Return Required[8]	Description of Organization
501(c)(1)	101(15)	None	Corporations Organized Under Act of Congress (including Federal Credit Unions)
501(c)(2)	101(14)	990[2]	Title Holding Corporation for Exempt Organization
501(c)(3)	101(6)	990[2] or 990-PF[3]	Religious, Educational, Charitable, Scientific, Literary, Testing for Public Safety, or Prevention of Cruelty to Children or Animals Organizations, or to Foster National or International Amateur Sports Competition
501(c)(4)	101(8)	990[2]	Civic Leagues, Social Welfare Organizations, and Local Associations of Employees
501(c)(5)	101(1)	990[2]	Labor, Agricultural, and Horticultural Organizations
501(c)(6)	101(7)	990[2]	Business Leagues, Chambers of Commerce, Real Estate Boards
501(c)(7)	101(9)	990[2]	Social and Recreation Clubs
501(c)(8)	101(3)	990[2]	Fraternal Beneficiary Societies and Associations
501(c)(9)	101(16) and (19)	990[2]	Voluntary Employees' Beneficiary Associations (including Federal Employees' Voluntary Beneficiary Associations formerly covered by section 501(c)(10))
501(c)(10)	N.A.	990[2]	Domestic Fraternal Societies and Associations
501(c)(11)	101(17)	990[2]	Teachers' Retirement Fund Associations
501(c)(12)	101(100)	990[2]	Benevolent Life Insurance Associations, Mutual Ditch or Irrigation Companies, Mutual or Cooperative Telephone Companies
501(c)(13)	101(5)	990[2]	Cemetery Companies

1. Generally if wholly or partially-owned by the federal government they are not subject to FUTA but are subject to FICA.
2. For exemptions see instructions Form 990. One exemption is for organizations with gross receipts of not more than $25,000.

(continued)

General Nature of Activities	Total Active Entities	Form No.[9]	Contributions Allowable	Subject to FICA & FUTA
Instrumentalities of the United States	17	No Form	Yes, if made for exclusively public purposes	Yes[1]
Holding title to property of an exempt organization	6,399	1024	No	Yes
Activities of nature implied by description of class of organization	548,976	1023	Generally, Yes	Yes[4]
Promotion of community welfare; charitable, educational or recreational	129,218	1024	Generally, No[5]	Yes
Educational or instructive, the purpose being to improve conditions of work, and to improve products and efficiency	65,086	1024	No	Yes
Improvement of business conditions of one or more lines of business	66,935	1024	No	Yes
Pleasure, recreation, social activities	57,905	1024	No	Yes
Lodge providing for payment of life, sickness, accident or other benefits to members	83,508	1024	Yes, if used for Sec. 501(c)(3) purposes	Yes
Providing for payment of life, sickness, accident or other benefits to members	13,801	1024	No	Yes
Lodge devoting its net earnings to charitable, fraternal, and other specified purposes. No life, sickness or accident benefits to members	20,829	1024	Yes, if used for Sec. 501(c)(3) purposes	Yes
Teachers' association for payment of retirement benefits	10	No Form[6]	No	Yes
Activities of a mutually beneficial nature similar to those implied by the description of class of organization	5,820	1024	No	Yes
Burials and incidental activities	8,772	1024	Generally, Yes	Yes

3. Public Charities must file Form 990 and Schedule A of Form 990 while Private Foundations must file Form 990-PF.
4. As of January 1, 1984, FICA coverage is mandatory. Prior to January 1, 1984, FICA Coverage is optional. Not subject to FUTA.

Types of Tax-Exempt Entities (continued)

Section of 1954 Code	Section of 1939 Code	Annual Return Required[8]	Description of Organization
501(c)(14)	101(4)	990[2]	State chartered Credit Unions, Mutual Reserve Funds
501(c)(15)	101(11)	990[2]	Mutual Insurance Companies or Associations
501(c)(16)	101(13)	990[2]	Cooperative Organizations to Finance Crop Operations
501(c)(17)	N.A.	990[2]	Supplemental Unemployment Benefit Trusts
501(c)(18)	N.A.	990[2]	Employee Funded Pension Trust (created before June 25, 1959)
501(c)(19)	N.A.	990[2]	Post or Organization of past or present members of the Armed Forces
501(c)(20)	N.A.	990[2]	Pre-paid Legal Service Funds
501(c)(21)	N.A.	990BL	Black Lung Benefit Trusts
501(c)(22)	N.A.	990[2]	Withdrawal Liability Payment Fund
501(c)(23)	N.A.	990[2]	Association of past or present members of the Armed Forces founded before 1880
501(d)	101(18)	1065	Religious and Apostolic Associations
501(e)	N.A.	990[2]	Cooperative Hospital Service Organizations
501(f)	N.A.	990[2]	Cooperative Service Organizations of Operating Educational Organizations
521(a)	101(12)	990-C	Farmers' Cooperatives Associations

5. Contributions to volunteer fire companies and similar organizations are deductible, but only if made for exclusively public purposes (Rev. Rul. 74-361, 1974-2 C.B. 159).

6. Application is by letter to the key District Director. A copy of the organizing document should be attached and the letter should be signed by an officer of the organization.

(continued)

General Nature of Activities	Total Active Entities	Form No.[9]	Contributions Allowable	Subject to FICA & FUTA
Loans to members. Exemptions as to building and loan associations and co-operative banks repealed by Revenue Act of 1951, affecting all years after 1951.	5,157	No Form[6]	No	Yes
Providing insurance to members substantially at cost	1,081	1024	No	Yes
Financing crop operations in conjunction with activities of a marketing or purchasing association	20	No Form[6]	No	Yes
Provides for payment of supplemental unemployment compensation benefits	546	1024	No	Yes
Payment of benefits under a pension plan funded by employees	4	No Form[6]	No	Yes
Activities implied by nature of organization	29,686	1024	Generally, No[7]	Yes
Legal services provided exclusively to employees	178	1024	No	Yes
Funded by Coal Mine Operators to satisfy their Liability for Disability for Death Due to Black Lung Disease	25	No Form[6]	No	Yes
To provide funds to meet the liability of employers withdrawing from a multi-employer pension fund	0	No Form[6]	No	Yes
To provide insurance and other benefits to veterans or their dependents	2	No Form[6]	Generally, No[7]	Yes
Regular business activities. Communal religious community	938	No Form	No	Yes
Performs cooperative services for hospitals	56	1023	Yes	Yes[4]
Performs collective investment services for educational organizations	1	1023	Yes	Yes[4]
Cooperative marketing and purchasing	1,695	1028	No	Yes

7. Contributions to organizations of past or present members of the Armed Forces are deductible only if 90% of the organization's members are war veterans.
8. Annual return required to be filed.
9. Form number for application for Recognition of exemption from income tax.

growing out of English Common Law that has been codified in many places around the country. Often there will be either an explicit limitation on suits or a prohibition altogether on the grounds that agencies funded by the public at large ought not to be siphoning resources into private hands via lawsuits. Liability considerations alone are not normally strong enough to determine a corporate structure, but the more favorable liability climate for public charities is clear.

The Role of the Internal Revenue Service

If programs sometimes seem fuzzily defined, there is no such problem with corporate structure. Unlike other forms of business organization, a corporation does not exist until certain governmental authorities say it exists. For nonprofit corporations, the lead voice in the chorus is the Internal Revenue Service. In matters having to do with nonprofit corporations, it is the IRS that giveth and the IRS that taketh away.

Corporations are organized according to the laws of individual states. Ordinarily, starting a corporation is as easy as filing the required paperwork and paying the necessary fees; in fact that is how all corporations must start. But government at all levels reserves the right to tax the profits of a business. In order to get the government to waive its right to tax—to allow a corporation to be *tax-exempt*—a would-be nonprofit corporation must show that it has been created and will be operated with certain purposes in mind. It must do so according to pre-established guidelines spelled out in the code. Then it must wait for the IRS' decision on the application.

IRS acceptance of exempt status is the turning point. After this step, state government often must have its say about the organization's acceptability as a tax-exempt entity. Normally state government is willing to follow the IRS' lead, so once the IRS has weighed in it's usually pro forma thereafter.

In effect, the IRS considers all nonprofits to be taxable entities until they prove otherwise. The major thing that distinguishes a nonprofit from a for-profit corporation is that most nonprofits (including all charities) are not allowed to have shareholders with whom to share profits. Note that this is not a prohibition against profits, just against having shareholders with whom to share them. This is the reason why it is often said that the profits of a nonprofit are kept within the corporation—salaries, benefits, and perks notwithstanding.

An IRS Question: Private Foundation or Not?

Historically, Congress has disliked private foundations, which are a form of charitable organization, probably because of the abuses that occurred when they were first "created." In 1969, the U.S. Congress laid the groundwork for what we now call private foundations. In the process of paying attention to private foundations, however, a curious thing happened. The IRS actually developed a much clearer and better developed sense of what a private foundation is than what a public charity is. Consequently, it essentially regards public charities as nonprofit corporations that are *not* private foundations. This is why the IRS letter granting tax-exempt public charity status says that the applicant is a tax-exempt corporation that is not a private foundation.

The driving force around which the determination of private foundation or public charity status revolves has nothing to do with public mission but rather is usually a product of that old-fashioned determinant, money and its control. Whereas a private foundation derives its initial or ongoing funding from limited private sources, regulators expect the charitable organization to get its funding from the public at large. For many public charities, that hurdle is set at one third of total revenue, although in a few obscure legal cases that percentage could be lower.

It is not hard to infer the authorities' motivation here. Private foundations' sole source of revenue being a single individual or family gives the founders tremendous control over determining who gets the benefits of the tax-exempt activity. It could also lead to a temptation to abuse that power if not kept in check. By obliging many public charities to derive a substantial chunk of their revenue from the public at large, the Congress has virtually guaranteed that a public charity's management could never exercise the same degree of control.

Another IRS Question: What Type of Nonprofit?

So far it may seem like the nonprofit organization's only choice about tax-exempt status is between private foundation and not a private foundation, but the range of choices is much broader than that. In fact, the familiar nonprofit public charity is only one of several possible options under which a nonprofit corporation can operate. In official IRS parlance, nonprofits are organized under Section 501(c) of the code. What all of these types of corporations have in common is that (1) they are exempt from federal and usually state corporate taxes and, in the case of public charities, (2) they are not private foundations. Significantly, only 501(c)(3) corporations—and a few others, under certain circumstances—can offer donors the right to deduct contributions from taxable income.

LOSS OF TAX-EXEMPT STATUS, OR THE MONSTER WITHIN

There is a monster loose in nonprofit land. It is a monster few have seen but many can describe, summoned up from nightmares to give body to commonly held, nameless fears. It has the power to terrorize whole boards of directors, senior staffs, attorneys, accountants, managers, and donors. It is the monster called "Loss of Tax-Exempt Status."

Like most monsters, this one's power comes not from what it does directly but from its ability to govern our thoughts and shape our actions in anticipation of encountering it. And it is in the latter dynamic that the uncritical mind is most vulnerable to the advice of those who would pretend to have glimpsed the beast.

Let us make the monster slink away into the night, discouraged by reality. According to the IRS, in 1992 the total number of those organizations that lost their tax-exempt status was 91. In 1991, it was 102.

If this surprises you as much as it surprised us, it might be well to remember that the business of managing the tax responsibilities of tax-exempt organizations is, at least at their initialization, largely a matter of trust. The IRS trusts that organizations that say they are organized to benefit the public good will do just that, and since the only return that they file (Form 990) doesn't determine the amount of money the government gets paid in taxes, there is little reason to systematically review it the way personal and for-profit corporate returns are handled (although the IRS does say that it examines a higher *percentage* of 990 returns than 1040 returns or

Changing Tax Status: A Case History

The designations of tax-exempt entity are categories in the tax code for which each corporation must apply. The IRS has the final word on whether a corporation fits any given category. Organizations can change their selection of code if their mission or activities change. One organization, an association of nonprofit providers, started life as a (501)(c)(3). Why? The founder was candid, "We knew the options, but foundation grants were going to be critical."

Over time the organization changed its identity from that of charity to one involving considerable lobbying on behalf of its member corporations and others like them. Nonprofit charities that begin to do substantial lobbying, in addition to having to pay a tax on lobbying above the allowable limits, must rethink their tax code election. The clock was ticking, because the IRS has the right to examine the organization's performance over a four-year period and revoke its public charity status if they determine that the corporation never operated in a proper fashion.

Eventually, the association chose to change its status from a 501(c)(3) public charity, to a 501(c)(4) social welfare organization. The tradeoff was explicit. In return for the opportunity to carry out considerable lobbying activity, the group lost its right to receive tax deductible contributions. In this case, there was no real problem because they had long ago ceased seeking foundation grants and because increased lobbying was clearly in support of its evolving mission.

1120s). To put it another way, there's no reason for the IRS to go looking for trouble in this sector.

Revocation Not Typical of Public Charities

When trouble finds the IRS and results in these yearly average 100 tax-exempt status revocations, it tends to fall disproportionately on groups that are not public charities. These organizations are social clubs, trade associations, fraternal organizations and the like that enjoy tax-exempt status but are not considered public charities in the same mode as the more familiar hospitals and universities.

In 1992, a total of 65 tax-exempt organizations that were not public charities lost their tax-exempt status. By far the biggest reason for exempt status revocation is that the corporations violated the prohibition against private inurement, meaning that they used their tax-exempt status to illegally enrich individuals connected with the organization in some way. Public charities also tend to lose their tax-exempt status for political work on behalf of individual candidates, a strictly prohibited activity. Another major reason for loss of tax-exempt status in all types of tax-exempt organizations is a group's receipt of an excessive amount of income from an unrelated trade or business.

Why should nonprofit board members care about IRS policy on tax-exempt status termination when so few organizations actually lose their privileged tax status? The answer to this question is rooted in the same reservoir of public trust and social spiritedness that gives rise to the privilege of tax-exemption in the first place. All of these are ways in which a tax-exempt organization behaves like something it is not, particularly when it acts as a vehicle for private enrichment.

The vast majority of nonprofit leaders are ethical, committed individuals who need not worry about their actions even remotely endangering the organization's tax-exempt status. This is the greatest counterbalance to the tiny fraction who would exploit the public trust.

But a more compelling and far more subtle reason for understanding the real risks regarding loss of tax-exempt status is to be in control of one's own organization. Citing a danger that doesn't exist, self-styled experts can exercise undue sway over the actions of a board or management team, insidiously discouraging the assumption of prudent risk or the exploration of innovative financial directions. Well-meaning advisors can work in monstrous ways.

CHAPTER TWO

Mission: Managing Your Two Bottom Lines

It has become popular to refer to the bottom line in contexts far beyond the merely financial. The phrase has a certain ring to it, a suggestion of no-nonsense that many find attractive. But the fact of the matter is that the bottom line isn't really, well, the bottom line. At least it isn't a bottom line in the sense of a definitive, live-or-die standard; any organization can lose money during any given year and still escape with relatively little damage. It can even do it several years in a row. For any kind of business entity, the real bottom line is the inability to get capital into the organization. For nonprofit corporations, that happens when no bank will loan any more money and no philanthropist will donate any more funds. For for-profits, it means no more credit, but it also means no one is willing to buy the stock anymore. Large nonprofit groups rarely go out of business because it is usually possible to persuade one more source of capital to contribute.

Profit is the organizing principle in the for-profit world. It is the only commonly shared arbiter of conflicts and the enduring benchmark of all activity. It forces the recognition that a particular course of action should be chosen because it is in everyone's best financial interests. At the same time, profit alone is a weak organizing principle because the economics affecting it can change so easily. Professional football teams win the Super Bowl one year and explode the next, their players and coaches picked over by rival teams willing to offer individuals money. Professional service firms constantly lose professionals who discover that they can make the same or greater profit offering the service on their own. Profit as a source of organizational discipline is the common strategy. Let's consider what alternatives serve when profit as a principle is missing.

THE ROLE OF A VALUE SYSTEM

Without profit as a factor, nonprofits must find another way to move the organization forward. Typically, they find it in a shared value system. Done properly, a shared set of values provides the kind of organizational discipline that the pursuit of profit would otherwise provide. For a variety of reasons it's not a perfect substitute, but as a lasting factor it is definitely superior. Incidentally, the very best for-profit corporations know the power of a coherent value system, and they know that it is stronger than the ups and downs of simple profit.

The role of shared values explains why certain nonprofit organizations can be contentious groups filled with infighting and rivalries. In a for-profit organization without a shared value system, sheer economics can carry things as long as times are good. But a nonprofit which loses its value system—often through a change in the executive director—has no such back-up. Strategic direction then becomes a matter of pitting one value system against another.

What does all of this have to do with managing the finances of a nonprofit corporation? The connection is simple yet powerful. Problems with finances mean problems accomplishing the mission. Missed payrolls mean dispirited, demoralized staff who cannot and will not give their service's consumers their full attention. A weak capital structure magnifies financial problems. Sluggish, inefficient systems retard growth, and so on. The very brightest of program service people cannot overcome poor financial performance and after a while they will resign. The opposite, however, is not true. Poor program performance can exist indefinitely in spite of good quality financial performance. Good financial health can actually prop up a programmatically bankrupt administration. Mediocre program results carry little financial penalty even when they cause reduced income because managers can always ratchet spending down to adjust. Failure in service delivery, except in intensively competitive arenas, usually implies less for finances than failure in finances implies for service delivery.

It is easy to see why. Financial failure is measurable and clearly understood by outsiders. Many outsiders pay attention to the finances, which have to be drawn up in a standardized way to permit comparisons. Bankers holding a nonprofit's mortgage are motivated to monitor fiscal performance. Funding sources regularly demand reports that can spotlight a financial problem. Institutional donors demand financial profiles. On the other hand, who will demand to see measurable outcomes of program services in most fields? And does anyone know what success would look like if it were achieved? The truth of the matter for some nonprofit services is that, from society's perspective, it is enough simply that the services exist and not that they be of some particular level of quality. Halfway houses for former offenders are a good example. The average citizen doesn't care much for the niceties of halfway house performance, just whether the program exists or not.

A former colleague of mine once spent a few years in the highest ranking administration and finance position in state government. Having come from a health care background, he was pleasantly surprised by the state highway construction and repair department's approach to its budget review. For their yearly budget, they would request x amount of dollars in order to pave y number of miles of roads according to z specifications that could be expected to last a certain number of years. The output and the cost might vary due to blips in the economy, but for the most part their projections were reliable. Budget decisions were a simple yes or no that would result in a predictable amount of work getting done.

Because there is no comparable measurement for most nonprofit programming, program failure goes unrecognized. Worse, it goes unpunished. In for-profit environments, the market rewards entities with profit and survival. With financial profit relegated to a lower priority, and with the exit door effectively blocked by a combination of legal, political, and cultural factors, there is no equivalent judge for nonprofits.

THE NONPROFIT'S DILEMMA AND
HOW TO SOLVE IT

These facts in combination with nonprofits' typical reasons for creation lead to nonprofits' central dilemma and suggest the way that good financial management can help resolve it. To begin, consider the following stories:

> Around the turn of the century, the leaders of a medium-sized factory town acknowledge a major social problem deriving from the very success that their town's many factories enjoy. The factories, working at full production with early industrial methods, are so unsafe that they routinely injure or kill employees. In turn, this creates a growing population of orphans that the town's social systems are unable to support. In need of a solution, the leaders reach out to a religious order hundreds of miles away and ask that they establish an orphanage in town. The order agrees. Eighty years later, the orphanage that the nuns created has grown into a health care system that includes three hospitals, two nursing homes, a home health care agency, and the original orphanage, which has now become a school for special needs children.

> During the nineteenth-century, state governments across the country began building large institutions for the mentally ill and mentally retarded. Over a hundred years later, for a variety of reasons including the institutions' high cost and inflexibility, they began to be replaced by networks of much smaller programs called community residences or group homes. Often operated by private nonprofit groups, these programs took as a cornerstone of their philosophy that care for their clients should be provided in the least restrictive setting possible, a direct criticism of the institutions the homes replaced.

Each of these vignettes illustrates in its own way a core truth of nonprofit organizations: Those that deal with the poor, the sick or the disabled very often come into being due to a dysfunction in some other part of society. Orphanages were needed due to a combination of factors such as workplace hazards, social conventions and economic pressures. When forces as diverse as federal laws, labor unions, governmental workplace regulation and birth control came into play, the demand for what we had called orphanages diminished. Ironically, many of those original orphanages have found a new role as educators of special needs children. Yet what are "special needs" students except those for which the conventional education system cannot or will not provide an education?

In these stories, we get a glimpse of the dilemma of nonprofit management: Organizations originally created to change society themselves become resistant to change *unless managed otherwise.* Unless, in other words, managers pay attention to their two bottom lines. And it is hard for most managers to meet one bottom line, let alone two. The result, in part, is the mild irony that nonprofit workers are often far readier to hold liberal views of the need for change in the external society than they are ready to accept changes in their own organization.

This resistance to change takes many forms, not all of them immediately recognizable as such. Some varieties masquerade as a commitment to "the community," or a fierce dedication to the client. This tendency to focus so narrowly makes the financial manager's job less complicated and therefore easier—a seductive prospect—but in the end it sells the mission short. Visiting nurse associations (VNA), for example, could have and should have dominated the home care field for much longer than they did, but when they got stuck in turf battles with similar agencies it allowed proprietaries to seize new markets and eventually the strategic advantage.

The VNA example also illustrates the way society must deal with whole industries that are unresponsive to change in either of their bottom lines. Society will demand services, and if any group of agencies is unmoved by the demands of either of its own bottom lines, society will create new organizations. Unfortunately, since the existing agencies rarely go out of business, the new and the old must exist together, in some cases sharing resources that are too lean to be shared. The lesson is that discipline must come from the financial bottom line, although not necessarily from the financial types.

The alternative is for program services to carve an unusually tough bottom line of its own, a very difficult task. One way to do this is through a philosophy I have called entrepreneurial nonprofit management. The essence of entrepreneurial management in the nonprofit sector is a commitment to creating opportunity for everyone associated with the organization, and a willingness to disregard conventional wisdom. A chief executive can accomplish the same thing through sheer force of will. But under normal circumstances, the likeliest source of influence over the organization is financial.

Nonprofit financial management carries a burden with a twist. It is not the sole nor even the most important reason for the organization's existence. If it stumbles over a sustained period of time, there is little hope that the organization will truly fulfill its mission. On the other hand, the corporation's success depends on its ability to steer program services away from fiscal irrelevance, and for this job it has to achieve and maintain internal clout. There really are two bottom lines in the nonprofit corporation, and finance owns the first one.

CHAPTER THREE

Balance Sheets: How They Get That Way

More than any other single financial report, the balance sheet is a window into the fiscal heart of the nonprofit corporation. In one concise accumulation of numbers, the balance sheet shows an impressive array of data about the results of virtually every fiscal policy the organization has ever pursued. Unfortunately, its trove of information is often concealed to the untrained eye. In this chapter, we scrape some of the frost off that window and help the ordinary observer make sense of what's inside.

The balance sheet is an ingenious device. On one side it places all the resources of an organization, its *assets*. On the other side it places the claims of outsiders against those resources, otherwise known as *liabilities*. Whatever is left over on that side is considered equity or, in the nonprofit world, net assets (formerly fund balance). This leftover is essentially a form of ownership claim against the assets. Adding up the assets gives you exactly the same amount as the sum of the liabilities and equities. Now you know why they call it a balance sheet.

Within the framework of assets equaling liabilities plus net assets there are very carefully defined categories. The rest of this chapter will explain those categories and how they behave. The numbers in parentheses refer to lines on the IRS Form 990. Exhibit 3.6 shows the IRS 990 form for an imaginary nonprofit organization, CCUA, that we will use in this and subsequent chapters.

CURRENT ASSETS

Although they're not labeled as such on the IRS 990, current assets are usually explicitly grouped as a multiple item category on audited statements. Current assets are defined as assets that could reasonably be expected to be turned into cash or consumed within a year. In certain for-profit businesses, the timeframe for current assets will be longer because the natural business cycle is longer (a distillery, for instance), but that is not much of an issue for nonprofits.

Cash (45)

Easy to understand—cash is the green and silver stuff. Mainly, however, cash is what's in the checkbook after it is fully reconciled.

Savings and Temporary Cash Investments (46)

Dollars parked somewhere for a short time. Certificates of deposit are a good example. These are also often called cash equivalents.

Accounts Receivable (47)

Some users of nonprofit organizations receive a service and then get billed for it. Those bills are official notices of money due the nonprofit. As such, they are worth something to the organization. Line 47 shows the total of all bills issued but not yet collected, called accounts receivable, or simply A/R.

Allowance for Doubtful Accounts (Same Line)

Even within organizations having good credit policies to prevent the delivery of services to customers who may not have the ability to pay, ultimately it may not be reasonable to expect all receivables to be collected. The amount of outstanding bills in this category is estimated in some sensible way by management and gets subtracted from the overall total of accounts receivable (A/R). This product is called the net accounts receivable and is entered in column B. In a slightly different context, those accounts that never materialize would be called bad debts.

Pledges Receivable (48)

Same principle as accounts receivable, except that these are promises by outsiders to make donations to the nonprofit that have not actually materialized yet. A June 1993 statement by the Financial Accounting Standards Board (FASB) stipulates new treatment for unconditional pledges received by a nonprofit organization. Effective for most organizations in their fiscal years that begin after December 15, 1994, FASB Standard No. 116 required nonprofits to recognize any unconditional pledge as an asset during the year in which it was made, no matter when the actual cash is received. Nonprofits will ultimately be showing more pledges as receivable, and many balance sheets will change significantly.

Grants Receivable (49)

Ditto, except that since pledges are made by individuals and grants by foundations, corporations, and government agencies, the latter usually don't produce many doubtful accounts. Reporting rules shouldn't change much here.

Receivables Due from Officers (50)

Occasionally—*very* occasionally, one hopes—nonprofits find it necessary to lend money to officers and directors. Since this kind of transaction depletes the resources available for the charitable mission, it can raise serious questions about the officers' execution of their fiduciary duties.

Other Notes and Loans Receivable (51)

Same principle as above, except that these are loans made to outsiders. Note the expectation that some of them will turn out to be doubtful in the same way as certain accounts receivable will be doubtful.

Inventories (52)

Only applicable in certain instances in the nonprofit world, inventories are the accumulation of raw materials, supplies, and the like that are waiting to be used in delivering services or making a product.

Prepaid Expenses and Deferred Charges (53)

These are, for the most part, benefits or expenses that have already been paid for and will be realized by the organization at some point in the future. Anyone who has ever paid a car insurance bill for a full year ahead of time understands a prepaid expense. Often this category includes things like the unused portions of the value of fully paid insurance policies that cross fiscal years.

Securities (54)

For those groups lucky enough to have them, securities are debt or equity financial instruments (stocks, for example) that produce income and can be sold to raise cash. When nonprofit corporations have a substantial endowment, this is usually how it's held.

NONCURRENT ASSETS

Assets in this category are harder to turn into cold cash on short notice. They're also nice assets to have, since they tend to be the kind that stick around for a long time.

Investments Held as Land, Buildings, and Equipment (55)

Self-explanatory, except that these items are normally shown at the cost of acquiring them (minus the appropriate depreciation), not at the price they would fetch on the open market. This is usually a big difference. These properties, unlike the ones on line 57, are held chiefly for investment purposes, not operations.

Other Investments (56)

It's perfectly legal for nonprofit organizations to make investments in for-profit companies. It may even be smart although that depends more on the investment acumen of the nonprofit's managers than on anything related to its tax status. Increasingly, universities, research outfits, and others make these types of investments. Line 56 is a bit different from line 54 in that it usually indicates an investment in nonpublicly traded financial instruments.

Land, Buildings, and Equipment (57)

Similar to line 55, except these are the operational holdings.

CURRENT LIABILITIES

Like their counterparts on the asset side, current liabilities are obligations the corporation owes within the next year. These are the most immediate claims against the assets.

Accounts Payable and Accrued Expenses (60)

Just as there are receivables that can be expected to be converted to cash, so there are bills owed that will have to be paid within the same timeframe.

Grants Payable (61)

For grant-making organizations, these payables were promised as of the date of the financial statements (or the tax return), but had not yet been disbursed.

NONCURRENT LIABILITIES

A bit less meaningful than noncurrent assets, noncurrent liabilities are still significant claims against the assets.

Support and Revenue Designated for Future Periods (62)

Sometimes an organization gets money explicitly intended for use after the end of the fiscal year. Three-year memberships, for instance, still have two years' worth of value left after the first year, so a portion of them is to be considered a liability and therefore not rightfully the nonprofit's at this point.

Loans from Officers and Directors (63)

The flip side of the transactions described in line 50.

Mortgages and Other Notes Payable (64)

Here is where to put all the long-term debt incurred in order to renovate that day care center or buy that headquarters building.

Fund Balances or Net Assets (67–74)

This is where it gets counterintuitive. First there's the matter of terminology. Like the word "profit," the term "net worth" in a nonprofit context has perhaps been considered too jarring for the average set of ears, so we have developed euphemisms like "fund balance" (again, due to FASB 117, fund balance is now known as "net assets"). No matter, it's the same thing.

Then there's the question of how the number gets calculated. Simple. If everything else has been accounted for and assets exceed liabilities, the amount it takes to get the two numbers identical is the fund balance/net assets. When liabilities exceed assets, the fund balance becomes negative and one has then arrived at what a diplomat might call an extremely worrisome deficit position that may be the prelude to bankruptcy. Big trouble, in short.

What is the fund balance or net assets? In essence, it is nothing more than the accumulation of surpluses or deficits the corporation achieved since its beginning. Extraordinary losses or gains aside, the net assets are the cumulative sum of all the year-end pluses or minuses since the organization started out in its current form. If the profits outweigh the losses, the net assets will be positive; otherwise, net assets are negative and it's dum-da-dum-dum time.

Now to completely confuse the matter. Managers will quickly pick up on the fact that one needs a healthy fund balance to remain a viable entity. Some who have studied the question briefly may even speak with pride about the size of the fund balance they maintain. All in all, one gets the clear impression of a fund balance as a positive thing, which is true, in the context of financial management. But some go on from there to assume that it's a positive thing in the same way that assets are positive things.

The truth is that the net assets are a form of claim against the assets of the nonprofit. Technically it's not the same as a liability, but for these purposes, it behaves similarly.

To put the question in a different light, think about who holds that claim. Let's start with a for-profit context. In a small business, the net assets equivalent would be "owner's equity" or "net worth." There the issue is much clearer. If the entity goes out of business and after final wrap-up the assets exceed the liabilities, the owner walks away with the equity.

In the nonprofit public charity world there can be no "owners" in the legal sense even though the accounting operates the same way. So the surrogate "owner" of a nonprofit's equity is . . . society. Seems fair. After all, society via its government has voluntarily agreed to refrain from taxing the profits made by this type of corporation with the expectation that it will do some public good in return.

The way this "ownership" gets operationalized is usually through the organization's legal incorporation papers that state something to the effect that if the corporation ever goes out of business any leftover assets will be distributed to similar groups. In practice this is little more than a theoretical nicety, if only because relatively few nonprofits ever actually go out of business. Also, the practical workings of a nonprofit dissolution tend to be overseen by a state official such as the attorney general and unless a case is highly visible the harried executive branch of state government tends to focus its energies elsewhere. Still, it's a nice metaphor. On the positive side, it embodies the best of a nonprofit's mission to serve the public. On the negative, it reminds us that there is at least theoretical accountability for the privileges of nonprofit status.

The fund balance or net assets is usually the hardest concept on the balance sheet to understand. This is probably because virtually every other item on the balance sheet can be traced to one or more pieces of paper in the accounting system. Cash deposits are documented in bank records, buildings have deeds, long-term liabilities have borrowing agreements. The fund balance, on the other hand, is an abstraction. It exists nowhere except on the financial statements, and it carries its greatest meaning in combination with some other quantity, as we will see in the chapter on diagnostic tools. All things considered, it is not an instinctively easy idea.

MAKING THE BALANCE SHEET DANCE

It's time now to see how a balance sheet behaves. Happily, it turns out to be an entirely predictable organism, not to mention a clever one. Take the simplified balance sheet in Exhibit 3.1 as a starting point. Remember that whatever we do to one side of the ledger has to be balanced completely with an equivalent cumulative change on the other side.

Assume for a moment that we want to buy another set of buildings for $1 million, putting down half of that amount and financing the other half. The transaction adds $1 million to the Land, Buildings, and Equipment account (call it LBE if you want to sound casually knowledgeable) and subtracts $500,000 from the cash account. Offsetting these are an increase of $500,000 in mortgage indebtedness as shown in Exhibit 3.2 (changed entries are in bold).

With a stroke of the pen and the help of financing, we have increased our asset base by half a million dollars. Notice that net assets did not increase because this was a financing transaction as opposed to a transaction that affected operations. The other half million simply transferred its place of residence from the cash account down to the LBE account when it was used as the down payment.

	Balance Sheet as of 12/31/9X (000s)		
Assets		*Liabilities and Fund Balance*	
Cash	$ 6,500	Accounts payable	$ 5,000
Accounts receivable	4,500	Mortgages	8,000
Land, buildings, & equipment	9,000	Other liabilities	2,000
		Net assets	5,000
		Total Liabilities and	
Total Assets	$20,000	Fund Balance	$20,000

Exhibit 3.1   Sample Balance Sheet

Balance Sheet as of 12/31/9X
(000s)

Assets		Liabilities and Fund Balance	
Cash	$ 6,000	Accounts payable	$ 5,000
Accounts receivable	4,500	Mortgages	8,500
Land, buildings, & equipment	10,000	Other liabilities	2,000
		Net assets	5,000
		Total Liabilities and	
Total Assets	$20,500	Net Assets	$20,500

Exhibit 3.2   Sample Balance Sheet with Purchase of Building

To go in a completely different direction, let's assume we have a nervous controller who doesn't like having bills sit around. He takes half of the available cash and pays off every bill he can find, leaving only a few that were hiding in the pipeline during his moment of madness. Starting with the original balance sheet, the new one looks like Exhibit 3.3.

Now let's go back to the original balance sheet and sprinkle efficiency dust over the billing system, causing $2 million of those original accounts receivable to be collected and not replaced. Watch the cash account balloon correspondingly in Exhibit 3.4.

Notice what doesn't change—everything else. Since improving the efficiency of the billing system meant getting the money owed to the organization sooner, that money went straight to the cash account. In effect, management transformed the form of the asset from one type (receivables) to another (cash). Since the measured

Balance Sheet as of 12/31/9X
(000s)

Assets		Liabilities and Fund Balance	
Cash	$ 3,250	Accounts payable	$ 1,750
Accounts receivable	4,500	Mortgages	8,000
Land, buildings, & equipment	9,000	Other liabilities	2,000
		Net assets	5,000
		Total Liabilities and	
Total Assets	$16,750	Net Assets	$16,750

Exhibit 3.3   Sample Balance Sheet with Paid Bills

Balance Sheet as of 12/31/9X
(000s)

Assets		Liabilities and Fund Balance	
Cash	$ 8,500	Accounts payable	$ 5,000
Accounts receivable	2,500	Mortgages	8,000
Land, buildings, & equipment	9,000	Other liabilities	2,000
		Net assets	5,000
		Total Liabilities and	
Total Assets	$20,000	Fund Balance	$20,000

Exhibit 3.4   Sample Balance Sheet with More Collected Funds

levels of all assets didn't change a bit, there was no need to do any-thing else to the other (liabilities) side of the balance sheet.

Finally, consider one way to make the fund balance swell. Imag-ine that the agency made a profit of $500,000 last year, and that, for the sake of simplicity, the final amounts of all balance sheet ac-counts stayed unchanged. That being the case, if revenue was $500,000 greater than expenses, it could only mean that the cash account increased by that number. Something else has to increase on the liability side by the same amount and, since all other things are assumed to be unchanged, it's the fund balance that will in-crease, as shown in Exhibit 3.5.

With the preceding as background, we can now get into the use-ful area of balance sheet diagnostics. It's possible to get a balance sheet (plus other parts of a financial statement) to give up some pretty impressive insights with only a little math; just another at-tribute of this most helpful of reports.

Balance Sheet as of 12/31/9X
(000s)

Assets		Liabilities and Fund Balance	
Cash	$ 7,000	Accounts payable	$ 5,000
Accounts receivable	4,500	Mortgages	8,000
Land, buildings, & equipment	9,000	Other liabilities	2,000
		Net assets	5,500
		Total Liabilities and	
Total Assets	$20,500	Fund Balance	$20,500

Exhibit 3.5   Sample Balance Sheet Showing the Effect of a Profit

Form **990**	**Return of Organization Exempt From Income Tax**	OMB No. 1545-0047
	Under section 501(c) of the Internal Revenue Code (except black lung benefit trust or private foundation) or section 4947(a)(1) nonexempt charitable trust	**1993**
Department of the Treasury Internal Revenue Service	Note: *The organization may have to use a copy of this return to satisfy state reporting requirements.*	This Form is Open to Public Inspection

A For the 1993 calendar year, OR tax year period beginning **JULY 1**, 1993, and ending **JUNE 30**, 19 **XX**

B Check if:	Please use IRS label or print or type. See Specific Instructions.	**C** Name of organization **CAMPAIGN TO CLEAN UP AMERICA**	**D** Employer identification number **44:4444444**
☐ Initial return			
☒ Final return		Number and street (or P.O. box if mail is not delivered to street address) Room/suite **1111 ANY STREET**	**E** State registration number **NONE**
☐ Amended return		City, town, or post office, state, and ZIP code **HOMETOWN, TEXAS 77777**	**F** Check ► ☐ if exemption application is pending
☐ Change of address			

G Type of organization—► ☐ Exempt under section 501(c)( ) ◄ (insert number) OR ► ☐ section 4947(a)(1) nonexempt charitable trust
Note: *Section 501(c)(3) exempt organizations and 4947(a)(1) nonexempt charitable trusts MUST attach a completed Schedule A (Form 990).*

H(a) Is this a group return filed for affiliates? . . . . ☐ Yes ☒ No

(b) If "Yes," enter the number of affiliates for which this return is filed:. . ►
(c) Is this a separate return filed by an organization covered by a group ruling? ☐ Yes ☒ No

I If either box in H is checked "Yes," enter four-digit group exemption number (GEN) ► ....
J Accounting method: ☐ Cash ☒ Accrual ☐ Other (specify) ►

K Check here ► ☐ if the organization's gross receipts are normally not more than $25,000. The organization need not file a return with the IRS; but if it received a Form 990 Package in the mail, it should file a return without financial data. **Some states require a complete return.**

Note: *Form 990-EZ may be used by organizations with gross receipts less than $100,000 and total assets less than $250,000 at end of year.*

Part I Statement of Revenue, Expenses, and Changes in Net Assets or Fund Balances

1	Contributions, gifts, grants, and similar amounts received:			
a	Direct public support	**1a**	599,110	
b	Indirect public support	**1b**		
c	Government contributions (grants)	**1c**	375,590	
d	**Total** (add lines 1a through 1c) (attach schedule—see instructions) (cash $ _____ noncash $ _____).		**1d**	974,700
2	Program service revenue including government fees and contracts (from Part VII, line 93)		**2**	37,700
3	Membership dues and assessments (see instructions)		**3**	
4	Interest on savings and temporary cash investments		**4**	5,000
5	Dividends and interest from securities		**5**	4,000
6a	Gross rents	**6a**	2,000	
b	Less: rental expenses	**6b**		
c	Net rental income or (loss) (subtract line 6b from line 6a)		**6c**	2,000
7	Other investment income (describe ►)		**7**	
8a	Gross amount from sale of assets other than inventory	(A) Securities **8a**	(B) Other	
b	Less: cost or other basis and sales expenses.	**8b**		
c	Gain or (loss) (attach schedule) . . ►	**8c**		
d	Net gain or (loss) (combine line 8c, columns (A) and (B))		**8d**	
9	Special events and activities (attach schedule—see instructions):			
a	Gross revenue (not including $ _____ of contributions reported on line 1a)	**9a**		
b	Less: direct expenses other than fundraising expenses . .	**9b**		
c	Net income or (loss) from special events (subtract line 9b from line 9a) .		**9c**	
10a	Gross sales of inventory, less returns and allowances . .	**10a**	40,000	
b	Less: cost of goods sold	**10b**	10,000	
c	Gross profit or (loss) from sales of inventory (attach schedule) (subtract line 10b from line 10a) .		**10c**	30,000
11	Other revenue (from Part VII, line 103)		**11**	
12	**Total revenue** (add lines 1d, 2, 3, 4, 5, 6c, 7, 8d, 9c, 10c, and 11) . . .		**12**	1,053,400
13	Program services (from line 44, column (B)—see instructions)		**13**	785,100
14	Management and general (from line 44, column (C)—see instructions)		**14**	130,800
15	Fundraising (from line 44, column (D)—see instructions)		**15**	103,500
16	Payments to affiliates (attach schedule—see instructions)		**16**	
17	**Total expenses** (add lines 16 and 44, column (A))		**17**	1,019,400
18	Excess or (deficit) for the year (subtract line 17 from line 12)		**18**	34,000
19	Net assets or fund balances at beginning of year (from line 74, column (A))		**19**	43,800
20	Other changes in net assets or fund balances (attach explanation) . . .		**20**	
21	Net assets or fund balances at end of year (combine lines 18, 19, and 20)		**21**	77,800

For Paperwork Reduction Act Notice, see page 1 of the separate instructions. Cat. No. 11282Y Form **990** (1993)

Exhibit 3.6 Sample IRS Form 990

Form 990 (1993)   CAMPAIGN TO CLEAN UP AMERICA   EIN# 44-4444444 Page 2

Part II Statement of Functional Expenses

All organizations must complete column (A). Columns (B), (C), and (D) are required for section 501(c)(3) and (4) organizations and section 4947(a)(1) nonexempt charitable trusts but optional for others. (See instructions.)

Do not include amounts reported on line 6b, 8b, 9b, 10b, or 16 of Part I.		(A) Total	(B) Program services	(C) Management and general	(D) Fundraising
22 Grants and allocations (attach schedule) (cash $_____ noncash $_____)	22				
23 Specific assistance to individuals (attach schedule)	23				
24 Benefits paid to or for members (attach schedule)	24				
25 Compensation of officers, directors, etc.	25				
26 Other salaries and wages	26	508,400	423,400	65,000	20,000
27 Pension plan contributions	27	5,000	5,000		
28 Other employee benefits	28	25,000	18,000	5,000	2,000
29 Payroll taxes	29	42,000	34,000	5,000	3,000
30 Professional fundraising fees	30	40,000			40,000
31 Accounting fees	31	10,000		10,000	
32 Legal fees	32	9,000		9,000	
33 Supplies	33	15,000	12,000	2,000	1,000
34 Telephone	34	28,000	22,000	4,000	2,000
35 Postage and shipping	35				
36 Occupancy	36	70,000	53,000	14,000	3,000
37 Equipment rental and maintenance	37	20,000	20,000		
38 Printing and publications	38	62,000	52,000	2,000	8,000
39 Travel	39	25,000	16,000	3,000	6,000
40 Conferences, conventions, and meetings	40	10,000	9,000	1,000	
41 Interest	41	1,000		1,000	
42 Depreciation, depletion, etc. (attach schedule)	42	26,000	24,700	800	500
43 Other expenses (itemize): a	43a				
b	43b	75,000	54,000	3,000	18,000
c	43c	5,000	2,000	3,000	
d	43d	28,000	26,000	2,000	
e	43e	15,000	14,000	1,000	
44 Total functional expenses (add lines 22 through 43) Organizations completing columns (B)-(D), carry these totals to lines 13-15	44	1,019,400	785,100	130,800	103,500

Reporting of Joint Costs.—Did you report in column (B) (Program services) any joint costs from a combined educational campaign and fundraising solicitation? ▶ ☐ Yes ☒ No

If "Yes," enter (i) the aggregate amount of these joint costs $_____; (ii) the amount allocated to Program services $_____; (iii) the amount allocated to Management and general $_____; and (iv) the amount allocated to Fundraising $_____.

Part III Statement of Program Service Accomplishments (See instructions.)

Describe what was achieved in carrying out the organization's exempt purposes. Fully describe the services provided; the number of persons benefited; or other relevant information for each program title. Section 501(c)(3) and (4) organizations and section 4947(a)(1) nonexempt charitable trusts must also enter the amount of grants and allocations to others.

Expenses (Required for 501(c)(3) and (4) organizations and 4947(a)(1) trusts; optional for others.)

a Volunteer Teams: To prevent litter and organize pick-up teams, the Campaign holds community meetings to recruit volunteers. Teams are provided equipment with which to clean up their communities. (Grants and allocations $_____)   252,900

b Public Education: Literature describing Campaign purposes to rid America of litter and clean up our cities, towns, and countrysides is prepared and distributed. Mailings, newspaper and magazine advertisements are used. (Grants and allocations $_____)   146,600

c Programs and Seminars: The Campaign sponsors educational meetings to bring together government officials, businesses and citizens to discuss new methods of trash collections, recycling, and litter reduction. (Grants and allocations $_____)   10,000

d The Campaign holds recycling contracts with 17 municipalities. Services range from weekly recycling pickups to special recycling events. (Grants and allocations $_____)   375,600

e Other program services (attach schedule) . . . (Grants and allocations $_____)   0

f Total (add lines a through e) (should equal line 44, column (B), Program services). ▶   785,100

Exhibit 3.6 Continued

Form 990 (1993) CAMPAIGN TO CLEAN UP AMERICA   EIN# 44-4444444   Page **3**

Part IV Balance Sheets

Note: Where required, attached schedules and amounts within the description column should be for end-of-year amounts only.		(A) Beginning of year		(B) End of year
Assets				
45	Cash—non-interest-bearing	12,000	45	29,000
46	Savings and temporary cash investments		46	
47a	Accounts receivable **47a** 149,800			
b	Less: allowance for doubtful accounts **47b** 10,000		47c	139,800
48a	Pledges receivable **48a**			
b	Less: allowance for doubtful accounts **48b**		48c	
49	Grants receivable		49	12,000
50	Receivables due from officers, directors, trustees, and key employees (attach schedule)		50	
51a	Other notes and loans receivable (attach schedule) **51a**			
b	Less: allowance for doubtful accounts **51b**		51c	
52	Inventories for sale or use		52	
53	Prepaid expenses and deferred charges		53	
54	Investments—securities (attach schedule)	19,000	54	10,000
55a	Investments—land, buildings, and equipment: basis **55a**			
b	Less: accumulated depreciation (attach schedule) **55b**		55c	
56	Investments—other (attach schedule)		56	
57a	Land, buildings, and equipment: basis **57a** 55,000			
b	Less: accumulated depreciation (attach schedule) **57b** 36,000	18,000	57c	19,000
58	Other assets (describe ▶ ___)		58	
59	**Total assets** (add lines 45 through 58) (must equal line 75)	49,000	59	209,800
Liabilities				
60	Accounts payable and accrued expenses	5,200	60	114,000
61	Grants payable		61	
62	Support and revenue designated for future periods (attach schedule)		62	18,000
63	Loans from officers, directors, trustees, and key employees (attach schedule).		63	
64a	Tax-exempt bond liabilities (attach schedule)		64a	
b	Mortgages and other notes payable (attach schedule)		64b	
65	Other liabilities (describe ▶ ___)		65	
66	**Total liabilities** (add lines 60 through 65)	5,200	66	132,000
Fund Balances or Net Assets				
Organizations that use fund accounting, check here ▶ ☒ and complete lines 67 through 70 and lines 74 and 75 (see instructions).				
67a	Current unrestricted fund	25,800	67a	56,800
b	Current restricted fund		67b	
68	Land, buildings, and equipment fund	18,000	68	21,000
69	Endowment fund		69	
70	Other funds (describe ▶ ___)		70	
Organizations that do not use fund accounting, check here ▶ ☐ and complete lines 71 through 75 (see instructions).				
71	Capital stock or trust principal		71	
72	Paid-in or capital surplus		72	
73	Retained earnings or accumulated income		73	
74	**Total fund balances or net assets** (add lines 67a through 70 OR lines 71 through 73; column (A) must equal line 19 and column (B) must equal line 21)	43,800	74	77,800
75	**Total liabilities and fund balances/net assets** (add lines 66 and 74)	49,000	75	209,800

Form 990 is available for public inspection and, for some people, serves as the primary or sole source of information about a particular organization. How the public perceives an organization in such cases may be determined by the information presented on its return. Therefore, please make sure the return is complete and accurate and fully describes the organization's programs and accomplishments.

Exhibit 3.6 Continued

CHAPTER FOUR

Financial Analysis: A Few Diagnostic Tools

Yes, you will need a calculator for this chapter. But not just yet, and when you do it will be pretty simple stuff. Before we get into the ratios themselves, try the simplest yet most insightful piece of financial analysis possible. Run your thumb down the asset side of the balance sheet and find the largest number. Make a mental note of it. You have just learned a tremendous amount about your organization. Because *whoever controls the single largest type of asset controls the organization.*

Here's why. Suppose the organization in question is a university, and the largest asset is the endowment fund (investments). Whoever controls those investments controls the university. Sure, the professors make curricula decisions, the president and the deans decide who to hire and promote, and so forth. But whoever controls the investments sets the conditions and shapes the environment in which those other players make their operational decisions. Shrink or expand the endowment and the money-generating power that goes along with it and you dramatically alter the circumstances under which those decisions are made.

Let's look at another example. A recycling program that holds the bulk of its assets as receivables from municipalities may be a free-standing operation, but it might as well add underneath the sign at its entrance "A wholly controlled subsidiary of local governments."

Although the following ratios cover a wide range of analysis, they are only a fraction of the ratios it is possible to calculate. What these particular ratios have in common is that they represent a good balance between analytical power and easy availability of the component numbers on the Form 990. Other diagnostic tools of the same or greater power may require a bit of inside information that does not have to be publicly disclosed. The intention of this chapter is to present a good set of tests that can be done by a total outsider to the organization as well as someone who has unlimited access to financial information.

FINANCIAL STATEMENT ANALYSIS FOR MATH PHOBICS

Math phobics, take heart. Crunching massive quantities of numbers isn't the only way to analyze a financial statement. In fact, you can learn a great deal about an organization without doing a single calculation. The secret lies in reading the words and knowing what they mean. Let's start from the beginning of the average financial statement.

Steps in Reading a Financial Statement

Professional financial analysts often follow these steps when reviewing an audited financial statement of a new organization.

- Read the opinion letter.
- Read all notes and internal opinion letters, if any (particularly true for OMB A-133 audits).
- Review the numbers in the format presented.
- (optional) Calculate financial ratios as desired.

Audit, Review, or Compilation?   Open the financial statement to the cover page, a letter signed by the CPA or CPA firm. The first verb you encounter tells you a lot. The sentence will go something like this: "We have (audited, reviewed, or compiled) the financial statements of XYZ Corporation . . ."

The difference between the three verbs tells the reader a great deal about the reliability of the financial statements. Technically, the financial statements are supposed to be the product of management, with the CPA's analysis of them offering three different levels of assurance. An audit is the highest form of reliability, since it involves careful analysis and testing of transactions according to the guidelines proscribed by various professional accounting societies and government regulators. A review, on the other hand, involves no such testing and merely suggests that the financial representations seem to make sense. Finally, a compilation is little more than a collecting and reformatting of raw financial records. Chapter Seven on choosing and using an auditor goes into greater detail on this subject.

The reader with a stake in the nonprofit will prefer an audited set of financial statements, and in fact many state and local governments—and most serious payers—require nonprofit agencies to obtain a full audit each year.

Before you leave this page, take a look at the date of the opinion letter. Compare it to the last day of the fiscal year. This date is the last day the auditors spent on the corporation's premises doing field work, and it can be a rough guide to how smoothly things went. If the date is more than three months or so after the end of the fiscal year, it could indicate that the books and records were so disorganized that the auditors had to spend extra time just getting things into shape before conducting the audit. It could also say something about the auditors' level of effectiveness. Either way, ask.

The Opinion　　The next place to look is toward the end of the cover letter where the text should read "In my (our) opinion, these statements present fairly . . . ." This is the sentence for which the agency obtained the audit, and if the word "except" appears anywhere in this sentence, or if the auditor declines to express an opinion, alarms should go off in your head. Unless the exception refers to technical accounting disagreements with the way certain information is presented, this is the auditor's place to reassure readers that things are pretty much as management says they are. As long as there are no exceptions or reservations expressed, the audit is considered to be an unqualified or "clean" opinion. Two of the most common reasons for qualified opinions are unspeakably bad records and the CPA's genuine fear that the organization may go out of business soon. Either one is cause for concern.

Now skip all of the pages with numbers on them and turn right to the notes at the back. The back pages are like a bulletin board where accounting rules and conventions demand that certain important information be placed. Here you'll find:

The Basis of Accounting   This note should say that the accrual basis of accounting was used in preparing the financials. There's just not much latitude here; nonprofit public charities simply ought to be using the accrual method of accounting, not the cash method. If there's a good reason why a nonprofit public charity should be using the cash method of accounting, we haven't thought of it yet. For more information on this subject, see the chapter on accounting.

Related-Party Transactions   Sometimes someone connected with the organization, say, on the board or the management team, will also enter into some sort of transaction with the corporation outside of his or her role. For instance, the CEO may own a piece of property which he or she rents to the corporation.

Related-party transactions can run the gamut from the perfectly innocuous to the sleazy. It's not always possible to tell which is which on the face of it, so accounting rules require that materially important related-party transactions be disclosed. Some funding sources require further detailed disclosure and some even attempt to eliminate all related-party transactions completely. This is going to be an area of increased scrutiny in the coming years.

Borrowing Practices   Accounting rules stipulate the long-term indebtedness be disclosed in some detail, so this area can be a gold mine of information, especially for nonprofits that have borrowed a lot of money. Pay special attention to:

- *Lines of Credit.* Essentially standing loans made by banks for balancing irregular cash flow in the short term. Is the line fully utilized as of the day of the statement? How much is it for? There are no real standards here, except to find out the purpose of the borrowing and compare it with the magnitude of the need.

- *Interest Rates.* Often the interest rate charged on borrowings says something about the organization. The prime rate is the interest rate banks charge their most favored customers, and few nonprofits fit that category, so you're likely to see a rate of "Prime plus" at least a percent. On the other hand, anything above approximately prime plus 1.75 percent may indicate lazy borrowing or a possible credit risk.

- *Purpose of the Borrowing.* The agency should match borrowing terms with purpose. That is, long-term borrowing should be used for long-term purposes such as investing in real estate, not supplementing cash flow.

- *Patterns of Long-Term Indebtedness.* Typically the footnotes will spell out future portions of long-term debt coming due. Since the year-by-year schedule of debt presents only what is currently obligated and does not include any planned long-term borrowing, the amounts shown should decline each of the future four or five years presented. If not, there may be a one time payment, or a "balloon" payment, coming due during one or more years. This is perfectly okay, but it should prompt the analyst to investigate the circumstances for the planned uptick in total long-term debt. Is it shrewd financing, or just putting off until tomorrow what they couldn't afford today?

- *Special Loan Covenants.* Occasionally a lender will attach specific requirements to a loan, such as that certain outstanding bills will be payable directly to the lender under certain circumstances. The agency may have had to agree to the provisions to borrow the money, but it will limit future flexibility to a greater or lesser extent.

Lawsuits Pending   If someone has filed suit against the agency, it could eventually mean a significant alteration in its financial health if the suit is successful. Readers of the financial statements need to know that a suit is pending, so that fact is disclosed in the footnotes. Management's evaluation of the suit, if it is strongly dismissive, may also be included. In any event, it's a disclosure that should prompt further questioning.

Extraordinary Transactions   Every now and then something just plain unusual—good or bad—will happen to each nonprofit organization. Here's the place to talk about it.

Pending Adjustments to Reimbursements, Rate Requests, and So On   In large nonprofits with complex reimbursement environments there are always financial questions that linger long after the books on a particular year have been closed. Although it may take an industry specialist to evaluate the specifics, it's still possible to infer something meaningful about the pattern of the adjustments or the sheer size of a rate adjustment request.

Uncertainty of Future Funding   If the auditors feel that the nature of the organization's funding is shaky but they're not ready to ring any alarm bells on the opinion page, they may slip in a phrase about how unreliable future revenue streams are—especially if the money comes from the government. It signals an area worth looking into.

Subsequent Events   If a major event occurs after the last day of the fiscal year being audited and it can be expected to have a material effect on next year's financials—again, either positive or negative—the auditors will make a note of it.

Reading the opinion letter and the notes from a set of audited financial statements will tell even the novice a considerable amount about the organization. The words of a financial statement operate on two levels. The first is the obvious content expressed. The second level is one open to veteran readers and can best be developed through experience. It consists of nuances such as the presence of an unexpected note or the cautious description of a pending lawsuit. Either one is accessible through simple reading—and not a single calculation.

Now it is time to get out your calculator and refer to Exhibit 3.6 on pages 35–39.   🖫

CURRENT RATIO

RATIO: Current Ratio
CATEGORY: Liquidity
FORMULA: $\dfrac{\text{Current Assets}}{\text{Current Liabilities}}$
FORM 990 FORMULA: $\dfrac{\text{sum of lines (45 to 54)}}{\text{sum of lines (60 to 63)}}$
SAMPLE RATIO: $\dfrac{(29,000 + 139,800 + 12,000 + 10,000)}{132,000} = 1.45$

The following ratios use column B (End of year) from the 990 balance sheet for all balance sheet calculations unless indicated otherwise.

What It Is

The current ratio is probably the most widely recognized measure of liquidity. This simple calculation—made easier since most audited financial statements have subtotals for both current assets and current liabilities—matches the short-term assets of an organization with the liabilities that it expects to face during the same period.

The power of this ratio lies in its simplicity. "Current" for most industries is defined as one year so, in effect, it selects a 365-day timeframe and asks, "During this period of time, how do the resources that can be converted to cash compare with the liabilities that we know will be coming due during the same period?"

What It Should Be

The conventional wisdom is that this ratio should be at least 2:1, that is, for every dollar of liabilities coming due there should be at least two dollars of assets available to pay them. Generally speaking, the higher the ratio the better—to a point. An excessively high current ratio can actually be a problem (and a sign of management timidity or inattentiveness) if it means that unneeded assets are being allowed to build up in short-term forms instead of being invested for longer term results. See Chapter Eight on cash flow management to determine how much cash should be readily available.

The nature of the nonprofit agency's need for cash is critical to a sensible interpretation of this ratio. Nonprofits with substantial amounts of complicated billing procedures need to have a stronger ability to meet short-term fluctuations in liabilities than those that get half of their revenues in cash at the door.

What It Is Not

This is actually a rather crude measure. Lumping a large number of asset categories into "current" masks the lack of meaningful liquidity that characterizes some of them. Inventories, for instance, do not typically get turned into cash easily—nor should the ongoing agency want to convert them, since they are presumably essential to continuing service delivery.

Fortunately, the inventory consideration is irrelevant for a large number of nonprofits and so the current ratio is as useful as anything one might need. For groups needing a more fine-tuned measure of liquidity where inventory is an issue, try the acid test:

$$\frac{\text{Cash} + \text{Marketable securities} + \text{Receivables}}{\text{Current liabilities}}$$

Working capital—you may have heard that phrase before—is simply current assets *minus* current liabilities.

DAYS' CASH

RATIO: Days' Cash
CATEGORY: Liquidity
FORMULA: $\dfrac{\text{Cash \& Equivalents} \times 365}{\text{Operating expenses} - \text{Depreciation}}$
FORM 990 FORMULA: $\dfrac{(45 + 46) \times 365}{(17 - 42)}$
SAMPLE RATIO: $\dfrac{(29,000) \times 365}{(1,019,400 - 26,000)} = 10 \text{ days}$

What It Is

Deprived of food, the human body proves surprisingly resilient. It slows its pace, shifts its focus, changes its systems. When the nourishment resumes, it readily returns to its former rhythms. The same is true for the nonprofit organization and its supply of cash. Deprived of cash, the entity adjusts its systems and compensates. This is a natural phenomenon, at least in a management sense, so the important question is, How long can it continue if the cash somehow gets completely shut off? The days' cash ratio gives that answer.

Think of days' cash as the number of days of average size cash disbursements the organization can withstand without any cash income. If a nonprofit spends $10,000 per day on average over a year and it has $200,000 of cash and cash equivalents on hand, it has 20 days' cash.

What It Should Be

To some extent, higher is better. However, by itself, the number doesn't tell us much, since it is pretty unlikely that incoming cash will be completely shut off for an extended period of time. What makes the number so useful is that it can be a good benchmark. In fact, the days' cash ratio is helpful mostly in the context of comparative analysis.

What this means is that industry norms are essential to full usage of days' cash calculations. While some clear-cut inferences can be drawn from the ratio in a vacuum—CCUA, for example, has little cash on hand by any measure—the deepest insights come from careful comparison with similar organizations. If nothing else, calculating this average helps focus management on how close to the bone their cash flow is running. Cash balances can be an eye opener, especially in a larger organization, but this number will cut through all of the fantasies and tell you exactly where you stand.

DAYS' RECEIVABLES

RATIO: Days' Receivables
CATEGORY: Liquidity
FORMULA: $\dfrac{\text{Accounts receivable} \times 365}{\text{Operating revenue}}$
FORM 990 FORMULA: $\dfrac{47c \times 365}{(1d + 2 + 3)^*}$
SAMPLE RATIO: $\dfrac{139{,}800 \times 365}{(974{,}700 + 37{,}700)} = 50$ days
*The idea here is to use only revenue sources that typically generate receivables. Lines 1 and 2 on the Form 990 also include grants, which typically are not considered receivable in the same way as invoices. However, "government grants" is a bit of an old-fashioned phrase that often means "government contracts," so it is usually safer to include line 1c. This part of the formula requires judgment.

What It Is

This is a multipurpose ratio if ever there was one. In one number, this measure not only says some very significant things about the size and nature of the bills owed to the organization at any one time, it also offers insight into the effectiveness of financial management systems as well as management philosophy.

To get the days' receivables, take the total amount of accounts receivable and divide it by the average amount of billings generated each of the 365 days of the year.

What It Should Be

Lower is better. Time is definitely money, and the less time it takes to collect one's bills the more cash one is likely to have on hand. In turn, that means more cash to be turned into another productive form of asset—such as investments—rather than being tied up in non-revenue producing receivables.

Days' receivables can offer a terrific window into management styles. A bloated number can mean bloated and inefficient billing systems (which probably implies some combination of: poor personnel preparation and supervision, weak administrative systems, inadequate computer technology, or inattentive management). On the other hand, there's some fine irony here. A ratio at or lower than the industry standard in an otherwise lackluster set of ratios can actually mean not efficient management but a desperate, hand-to-mouth, beg-the-clients-we've-got-a-payroll-to-meet-tomorrow style of management.

Campaign to Clean-Up America (CCUA) sets a poor example by almost any standards, with a days' receivables ratio of nearly three months. On the other hand, a bit of careful reading reveals that they contract with 17 municipalities for recycling work. If that project produces most of the receivables, and that's a good guess, then at least the damage is confined to that single program.

A tip. Ballooning accounts receivable represent one of the best areas for a new manager to make fast progress in halting a financial slide. Most agencies have little or no idea how long it takes them to collect their bills, and many don't understand how necessary it is to care. Or rather, they don't sense how important it is to keep receivables under control. Sometimes all it takes to improve the situation is to begin tracking the days in receivables (also called the collection period) and to set a lower target for the chief financial officer to hit.

What It Is Not

As presented, the days' receivables doesn't reveal anything about the quality of the bills. For that, one needs: (a) access to the internal records, and (b) knowledge of the industry. To some extent one can count on the organization's auditors to insist that receivables that will never be collected get thrown out of the total count, but if the auditors don't understand the industry—or if management is determined to finesse them—the total amount of accounts receivable will be inflated.

CASH FLOW TO TOTAL DEBT

RATIO: Cash Flow to Total Debt
CATEGORY: Capital
FORMULA: $\dfrac{\text{Net income} + \text{Depreciation}}{\text{Total liabilities}}$
FORM 990 FORMULA: $\dfrac{18 + 42a}{66B}$
SAMPLE RATIO: $\dfrac{34,000 + 26,000}{132,000} = 0.45$

What It Is

Having liabilities means being obligated to pay them off. One of the quickest tests to use to understand something about the nonprofit's capital structure is the contrast between profit and depreciation as sources of cash and total liabilities. This ratio puts a slightly different twist on the idea of internally generated cash. What it asks is how much free cash is available each year to satisfy the liabilities on record. As will be seen in later chapters, profit creates cash for the nonprofit. Since depreciation is an expense that is not paid for in cash, it too leaves cash in the organization. Together, these two sources of cash are measured against the total liabilities of the organization.

What It Should Be

Higher is better. This is one ratio where most nonprofits will not score high because their net incomes are usually relatively low. Still, profit and depreciation are inescapable sources of cash regardless of tax status, so the ratio is a fair indicator of capital structure.

DEBT TO FUND BALANCE (NET ASSETS)

RATIO: Debt to Fund Balance (Net Assets)
CATEGORY: Capital
FORMULA: $\dfrac{\text{Long-term liabilities}}{\text{Net assets}}$
FORM 990 FORMULA: $\dfrac{64a + b}{74}$
SAMPLE RATIO: $\dfrac{0}{77{,}800} = \text{NA}$

Note: To get a more precise number, add the end of the year's net assets to the prior year's net assets and divide by 2. This gives a more accurate picture of the average net assets.

What It Is

Straight from the for-profit world (where fund balance or net assets means equity), this ratio says something about the amount of long-term indebtedness an agency carries in order to do its business. Long-term debt means money loaned for any purpose with a payback period longer than one year, so the debt/fund balance ratio stacks an organization's total indebtedness against its accumulated net worth, or fund balance. Another way to think about it is that it pits borrowed funds against "owned" funds. If an organization is highly leveraged—meaning that it has borrowed lots of money—you'll see it here.

What It Should Be

This one is important for itself. Lower numbers indicate low debt loads. Since the number is expressed as a percentage, it's easy to compare it with other nonprofits' debt/fund balance ratios. Industry ratios help put the answer in perspective, but the heart of the question is simply how high the number goes.

Perhaps not surprisingly, the best results here are well under 1.00. Accumulated wealth is not as desirable in a nonprofit setting as it is in a proprietary one, yet it's still nice to know that the total amount borrowed is less than the corporation's "net worth." CCUA is doing quite well in this department, with no long-term debt.

Again, some careful interpretation is necessary. Many nonprofits operate in fields where little capital investment is required, so the debt/fund balance ratio should be low and even irrelevant. Sometimes the board is debt-shy and refuses to authorize any long-term debt if they can possibly avoid it. Other groups must invest heavily in equipment and usually have to borrow to do it, so the issue for them is more like the nature of the debt and how one nonprofit's debt load compares to its peers.

The other consideration here is what happens to this ratio over time. Look for the relationship between this ratio and the strategic direction of the organization. If conditions warrant expansion, expect the number to increase, probably for several years. If debt is declining or gets restructured, you'll also see some change. Remember that a significant change in *either* direction in debt load will translate into a significant increase or decrease in the dollars paid out of operations for interest.

Incidentally, you can reverse this ratio and get an equally useful number showing how many times the fund balance covers the long-term debt level.

TOTAL MARGIN

RATIO: Total Margin
CATEGORY: Profitability
FORMULA: $\dfrac{\text{Revenue} - \text{Expenses}}{\text{Revenue}}$
FORM 990 FORMULA: $\dfrac{18}{12}$
SAMPLE RATIO: $\dfrac{34,000}{1,053,400} = 3.2\%$

What It Is

This is the bottom line, the one editorial writers point to with gusto, the one that tough, no-nonsense managers of all stripes supposedly focus on single-mindedly. It's what is left over after subtracting all the expenses from all the revenue, then dividing that number by all the revenue. It's the fundamental profitability indicator, and the IRS requires you to show half the math just by filling out the Form 990 anyway.

What It Should Be

Higher is better, up to a point. While most nonprofit managers now recognize the necessity of at least trying to turn a profit each year, that accomplishment is merely a condition of nonprofit business, not the purpose of it.

The logical question is, "How much profit is enough?" The answer is, "What do you need it for?" Since most types of nonprofit corporations can't sell stock and since most foundations are not keen on the idea of contributing working capital (to put it mildly), profit is one of the few ways that the organizations can generate cash for investment, innovation, or capitalization. Generally speaking, the more stable and unchanging the organization, the less there is a need for profit. Nonprofits planning expansion, new ventures, or just trying to build a more reliable future will need higher total margins. Specific industry standards, if available, will give excellent guidance on exactly how much profitability similar groups enjoy.

OPERATING MARGIN

RATIO: Operating Margin
CATEGORY: Profitability
FORMULA: $$\frac{\text{Operating revenue} - \text{Operating expense}}{\text{Operating revenue}}$$
FORM 990 FORMULA: $\dfrac{(1d + 2 + 3) - (13 + 14)}{(1d + 2 + 3)}$
SAMPLE RATIO: $$\frac{(974{,}700 + 37{,}700) - (785{,}100 + 130{,}800)}{(974{,}700 + 37{,}700)} = 9.5\%$$

What It Is

Push to the next level of analysis by calculating the operating margin. As useful as it is, the total margin can disguise some critical things going on in the organization. For instance, one organization experienced a giant deficit one year. Fortunately for them, that was the same year that some recently departed soul left them a more than giant bequest. One more than giant bequest minus one giant deficit equals one small profit. For one year, at least. But such good fortune masked a problem with their underlying economics that the operating ratio would have revealed.

What this ratio asks is that we compare all the revenue derived from operations against all the expenses associated with those operations. This means eliminating any revenue gained from fundraising as well as dividends, extraordinary income, and so on. To be fair, it also means eliminating identifiable expenses associated with that fund-raising. Sometimes this subtlety is not possible because data the outsider gets often does not separate out fund-raising expenses reliably (although the Form 990 does). This will tell us the true profit, minus all of that fund-raising noise.

What It Should Be

There's a funny thing about this ratio; old-timers, especially those serving on boards, often feel proud of a high level of fund-raising (i.e., a negative operating margin). And, indeed, doing a substantial amount of fund-raising is something to be proud about. But it means that the agency is extremely dependent on its contributors. Looked at another way, whoever contributes the operating revenue is unwilling or unable to pay full freight. The continued existence of the services is at the mercy of the tastes—and means—of those third-party contributors.

The answer to this dilemma only sounds evasive: The operating margin should be exactly where the organization wants it to be. Either the corporation willingly relies on fund-raising to supplement a chronically negative operating margin, or it uses fundraising to pay for the difference between merely good programs and great ones. It's an individual choice—no one size fits all—but it should be a conscious, deliberate choice.

RETURN ON FUND BALANCE (NET ASSETS)

RATIO: Return on Fund Balance (Net Assets)
CATEGORY: Profitability
FORMULA: $\dfrac{\text{Total revenue} - \text{Total expenses}}{\text{Avg. net assets}}$
FORM 990 FORMULA: $\dfrac{18}{(74B + 74A)/2}$
SAMPLE RATIO: $\dfrac{34{,}000}{(77{,}800 + 43{,}800)/2} = 55.9\%$

What It Is

This one is firmly in the category of "Let's Pretend" since it is nothing more than a knock-off of a classic for-profit measure. If the fund balance is essentially a measure of the accumulated profits the organization has made (and held onto), and if the leftover revenue after expenses is the bottom line for any given year, then setting the bottom line against the fund balance suggests how efficiently the fund balance has created that year's profit.

Think of the fund balance as being "owned" by the same public that grants the nonprofit its tax exempt status. Making that translation, it's fair to ask how successful the agency's management has been at creating a profit when compared with the fund balance with which they were given to work.

What It Should Be

Everything that is true of the total margin ratio is true of the return on fund balance, since it is just another way of examining net overall profit.

What It Is Not

Proprietary owners take this ratio seriously, calling it a return on equity, or something like that. Since the sky's the limit for total margin in a for-profit, while different incentives apply in nonprofits, it's not a fair comparison. Still, it suggests something about how the nonprofit regards its task. Used sparingly, it can yield some real insight.

ACCOUNTING AGE OF PLANT/EQUIPMENT

RATIO: Accounting Age of Plant/Equipment
CATEGORY: Miscellaneous
FORMULA: $\dfrac{\text{Accumulated depreciation}}{\text{Depreciation expense}}$
FORM 990 FORMULA: $\dfrac{57b}{42a}$
SAMPLE RATIO: $\dfrac{36,000}{26,000} = 1.38$ years

What It Is

Imagine being able to read a set of financial statements in Atlanta and describe the qualitative aspects of a nonprofit's buildings and equipment in Oregon—and be right 90 percent of the time! This little trick gives you some special insight into a major aspect of a nonprofit's financial profile.

Average accounting age of plant is a pure index, even though it is measured in "years." Assets are always depreciating (i.e., wearing out), so dividing the total depreciation charged on the current tangible asset inventory by the amount charged in any one year gives an idea of how young or old the property, plant, and equipment is.

What It Should Be

Lower is better. What's really being measured is not age per se, but the rate at which plant and equipment get used up and replaced. This is another ratio that will tell you something about the organization in isolation, and even more in comparison with others in the same general area.

Knowing what it takes to get the nonprofit's job done is the starting point for making use of this calculation. Hospitals, for instance, must invest in expensive equipment and keep their large buildings in good repair just to stay even with the changes in medical technology, so this is a particularly telling number for them. Success in this area means better positioning to attract the best physicians, which means more referrals, which means more revenue. Failure to keep one's investment program current even for a few years in this type of environment may take its worst toll several years later and can quickly lead to the erosion of operating results.

What It Is Not

Little depreciation activity doesn't allow the analyst to draw meaningful conclusions, except to venture the safe guess that the organization rents all of its sites (which could be inferred from the lack of any entry on line 57a of the Form 990 anyway). It also doesn't allow you to separate out the mix of items producing the depreciation charges, so a very old hospital building could boost the number artificially even if all the equipment had come out of the box yesterday.

A FOOTNOTE

Ratios can give enormously powerful insight into a nonprofit's financial well being. Rarely does a single ratio offer reliable insight, but an integrated package can do just that, painting a picture of financial health that can be quite revealing. Most of these ratios are at their best when compared with something else such as a target value, a previous year's value, or an industry standard. Unfortunately, industry standards are hard to acquire for nonprofits. The lack of uniformity in programming, an historic lack of appreciation for the power of quantitative comparisons, and lagging computer technologies are just some of the reasons why standards don't exist in large numbers.

Happily, the picture is changing. More and more managers are beginning to realize the value of benchmarks such as these, and logical suppliers of industry averages such as associations, universities, and financial advisors are beginning to provide them. It may very well be possible to obtain meaningful local standards from one of these types of sources. Even in their absence, however, it is worth calculating the amounts solely for internal purposes.

PART TWO

Accounting

CHAPTER FIVE

Nonprofit Accounting: Acknowledging the Strings Attached

If the measurement of profitability recedes as a driving force for nonprofit accounting, accountability comes to the foreground. Entities whose mission is to make a profit for their owners do not have to care very much about where their money comes from or how it is used, except for some fairly broad requirements imposed by lenders or the rules of securities exchange. By contrast, nonprofit corporations often need to be scrupulous about tracing both aspects of a transaction. Beginning in 1994, the way that organizations did that began to change significantly due to the adoption of FASB 117, a pronouncement governing nonprofits' financial statements.

Prior to 1994, a practice called fund accounting evolved to fulfill the more stringent standards of nonprofit accountability. In financial terms, it was the single greatest inherent difference between the two sectors in accounting and financial management. The term "fund accounting" refers to a loose collection of practices typically found in tax-exempt organizations. Five separate groups within the tax-exempt field developed their own versions of fund accounting: government, hospitals, colleges and universities, health and human services agencies, and a mix of miscellaneous tax-exempt entities.

Initial efforts at standardization occurred within each of these categories, leading to a patchwork of accounting practices. Of the five, government fund accounting grew so complex and self-referencing over the last three decades that in the 1980s it became a separate category of accounting in itself, with its rule-making and standard-setting functions separated from those of commercial accounting and the rest of fund-accounting users.

THE NEW FUND CATEGORIES

According to FASB, the purpose of Statement 117 is to "enhance the relevance, understandability, and comparability of financial statements issued by" nonprofit organizations. The pivotal consideration for 117 is the presence or absence of donor restrictions, that is, the strings attached to a nonprofit's resources. The explicit intention of FASB 117 was to make nonprofit financial statements as readable and usable by stakeholders of the nonprofit organization as they are for commercial entities. It was effectively a recognition that former accounting practices in this field were more restrictive —and for no identifiably productive purpose —than in the commercial sector.

Before FASB 117, there were five or more groupings of funds, as well as a potentially confusing presentation of the financial statements that had the effect of fragmenting the overall financial picture of the organization and making it difficult to get a coherent picture of its financial health. Now there are only three funds: (1) permanently restricted; (2) temporarily restricted; and (3) unrestricted. Further, these groupings apply only to the net assets (formerly fund balance) of the organization.

Permanently Restricted Net Assets (Fund Balance)

These are the portion of net assets that result from contributions or other types of inflow of assets whose use is limited by restrictions placed by the original donor. For an asset to be permanently restricted, there needs to be a condition imposed by the donor that can never be met or that simply does not expire with the passage of time. Net assets can also be permanently restricted as a result of reclassification of other classes of net assets due to donor requirements.

Temporarily Restricted Net Assets (Fund Balance)

Net assets are classified in this fashion if it can reasonably be expected that the organization can meet the donor-imposed conditions or that the restrictions simply expire after a certain period of time.

Unrestricted Net Assets (Fund Balance)

This portion of net assets is unencumbered by any restrictions placed by donors and can therefore by used freely by the nonprofit.

OTHER PROVISIONS

FASB 117 also attempts to standardize nonprofit financial reporting by defining what should go into the financial statements. Previously, there was a great deal of variability in the way that nonprofit organizations reported such things as cash flows and expenses. Now, a complete set of financial statements is defined as including:

- A statement of financial position (balance sheet)
- A statement of activities (changes in net assets)
- A statement of cash flows
- Accompanying notes
- A statement of functional expenses (voluntary health and welfare organizations only).

FASB 117 took effect for all nonprofits whose fiscal years began after December 15, 1994. Implementation of the statement was delayed for fiscal years beginning after December 15, 1995, for organizations with less than $5 million in total assets and under $1 million in annual expenses. In effect, all nonprofit financial statements issued during 1997 and later will be governed by FASB 117.

WHAT IT ALL MEANS

The effect of fund accounting was to treat each of these fund groups as though it were its own separate entity, with separate assets, liabilities, and fund balances. The sum of the five (or fewer) for each organization was the total for the corporation as a whole.

Exhibit 5.1 shows a highly simplified presentation of a balance sheet under fund accounting for a hypothetical organization. Exhibit 5.2 shows the same balance sheet presented according to the stipulations of FASB 117.

The difference is clear, even to the untrained eye. Fund accounting was complex and hard to follow and focused much more on the component parts of an agency's finances, all to get a precise picture of how the funds with strings attached have been used. The new statements, on the other hand, treat the organization as a whole entity and only spell out restrictions for net assets. One hopes that this relatively small but very significant alteration will encourage everyone to view nonprofits as integrated, whole organizations rather than as the sum of many smaller parts.

Having said all that, we must draw a distinction between the evolving nature of external reporting governed by FASB 117 and the internal needs of management. Because of the frequent demands of funding sources to account for their particular donation, nonprofit accounting must be capable of "drilling down" to the level where the funds are being used, that is, the program level. Health and welfare agencies would continue to report expenses by their natural classifications in a matrix (i.e., spreadsheet-like) format.

This higher level of accountability, the equivalent of Ford Motor Company routinely making detailed revenue and expense information available for its Taurus line of automobiles, comes at a price. One element of the price is that a nonprofit's accounting system needs to be able to handle that additional dimension, which tends to make it more expensive than systems that need to deal only with the corporate level.

A second element of the additional cost is that one must be able to allocate costs fairly and efficiently across the board. For example, if an individual is in charge of two programs, the accounting system must be able to reflect the fact that the cost of paying the individual should be spread across two programs. For-profit corporations have the same kind of need, but in that context it is called a *cost accounting system*. It is usually in place to support the pricing function without any of the legal and public accountability built into the average nonprofit's financial reports.

The complications of financial accountability do not stop here. Programs rarely have a single funding source, and those programs

	Unrestricted	Restricted	Land, Building, & Equipment	Endowment	Trust	Total All Funds
Assets						
Cash	$100,000	$10,000		$ 500,000	$50,000	$ 660,000
Accounts receivable	75,000					75,000
Securities				3,000,000		3,000,000
Land, building, & equipment			500,000			500,000
	$175,000	$10,000	$500,000	$3,500,000	$50,000	$4,235,000
Liabilities						
Accounts payable	$ 50,000				$50,000	$ 100,000
Notes payable	125,000					125,000
Long-term debt			400,000			400,000
Fund balance		10,000	100,000	3,500,000		3,610,000
	$175,000	$10,000	$500,000	$3,500,000	$50,000	$4,235,000

Exhibit 5.1 Nonprofit Balance Sheet—Fund Accounting Pre-FASB 117

Assets	Total
Cash	$ 660,000
Accounts receivable	75,000
Securities	3,000,000
Land, building & equipment	500,000
	$4,235,000

Liabilities	Total
Accounts payable	$ 100,000
Notes payable	125,000
Long term debt	400,000
Net assets	
Unrestricted	3,600,000
Temporarily restricted	2,500
Permanently restricted	7,500
	$4,235,000

Exhibit 5.2   Nonprofit Balance Sheet after FASB 117

with multiple funding sources need to match some portion of program funding with some portion of program expenses. In short, because there is a second level of data gathering and reporting, there must be a third level, as follows:

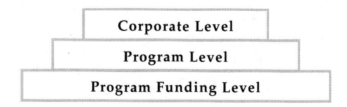

The interaction between program funding level information needs and the nature of nonprofit accounting itself give nonprofit organizations the characteristics of operating as though they were a collection of independent businesses. That sense of independent internal entities is actually pretty close to the mark and was encouraged by traditional fund accounting. It is also one of the reasons why accounting software developers were so slow to develop packages that could serve nonprofit users.

One side effect of the need for program-funding level accountability is that it sets a good foundation for management accountability as well. The chapter on management controls explains this idea further.

A negative side effect is that it complicates the accounting task. A for-profit company with two or three different products producing a million dollars of revenue will probably have internal financial statements that do not distinguish between the products in any way. For that type of information, they would have to rely either on a cost accounting system or, more likely, the general manager's intuitive sense and a few quick calculations by the bookkeeper. A comparable nonprofit, on the other hand, would be likely to have to report its expenses and probably its revenues by program at some point, which means that its accounting system for the same revenue level would have to be relatively more sophisticated.

To make things more complicated, the most scrutinized spending area is typically personnel. As long as a given individual works in only one program, his or her expenses can be charged directly to that program. But as soon as one individual is assigned to two or more programs, his or her overall cost has to be shared ("allocated") among the programs, and the task gets complicated.

Devising a reasonable and workable set of allocations and maintaining them is difficult enough under any circumstances, but if the accounting system is flawed in any way, the job could be hopelessly muddied. One $2.5 million antipoverty agency had several thousands of dollars in questioned costs as a result of one audit. The problem was that they had faithfully kept time and attendance records to support the payroll, but at some point a year's worth of allocation formulas and worksheets had disappeared.

Although they could prove that employees had in fact worked the hours that they were reported to have worked, using attendance records, they couldn't reconstruct how employees who crossed program lines had been allocated. Ninety-five percent of the total revenues came from government, and the auditors never questioned whether payroll payments had been made as recorded. The only reason the costs were questioned was because the organization was unable to show how it allocated costs to the various government funding sources. Ultimately, the organization encountered serious problems with their government funders which have yet to be resolved as of this writing.

Recent changes in nonprofit accounting hold the promise of simplifying a previously complicated reporting style. Policy makers in the field have begun to act on the recognition that nonprofit financial statements should convey useful information similarly to their for-profit counterparts. There will almost certainly be transition pains, but ultimately the changes should prove worthwhile. In any case, the strings-attached nature of nonprofit accounting, especially for public charities, will continue to demand a relatively higher degree of financial sophistication than that typically necessary in the commercial world.

CHAPTER SIX

Cost Accounting: How Much Does It Cost?

How much does it cost to provide your services? There are many answers. But the one thing that all responses to the question have in common is that they must first answer the equally important question, "Who cares?"

The theoretical answer to this resonant question is easier than the practical one. Speaking from the moral high ground, everyone connected with a nonprofit has a reason for caring about the cost of services in order to make sure that they are delivered as efficiently as possible. Certainly boards of directors should know the true cost of services as part of their fiduciary responsibility.

In practical terms, however, the real answer to the question "Who cares?" is rooted in economics rather than the public good. As a result, some nonprofits must care a great deal about the cost of their services while others feel no economic pressure to do so. Generalizing about which type of organizations respond in which way is hard, but during the 1990s, health care and cultural organizations tended to be the ones most heavily pressured as revenues turned shaky.

For any nonprofit, there are many reasons beyond the moral and narrowly financial to have some type of cost accounting information. To the extent that any proposed programming resembles an existing service, it is always extremely helpful to have cost information while building a planned budget. Cost information allows comparisons between services both inside and outside of the nonprofit organization. It can also be useful for political and grant-winning purposes to be able to show an actual cost per unit of service delivered.

In the past, especially in health and human services, cost accounting was important because of the way it produced information requested by government purchasers in order to set rates. The implicit assumption was that providers would be nonprofit, and, unlike for-profit companies, they would only be concerned with recouping their costs.

With the rise of simplified, prospective payment systems, the role of cost accounting as the source of compliance with regulations has diminished but, ironically, management has begun to value it more as a tool for internal decision making. Did a particular program make money last year? Why or why not? If we keep a losing program open, what will it do to our budget? Why are these two very similar contracts' costs behaving so differently? Cost accounting can help answer questions like these, and it can also provide the raw material for much deeper analyses. Even if a nonprofit gets all of its funding from noncontract sources, it will have to have a good understanding of its cost structure to succeed in the future.

A FORM OF MANAGEMENT ACCOUNTING

Cost accounting is a form of management accounting. In order to do it right, the underlying financial accounting must be sound. One of the distinguishing features of financial accounting is that its records are or could potentially be subject to verification. Cost accounting, on the other hand, while its mechanics are just as mathematical and logical as financial accounting, rests on concepts that tend to be unique to an institution. For that reason, cost accounting information rarely has much meaning outside of an organization unless the definition and treatment of costs are standardized.

Cost accounting would be a lot simpler if the only costs incurred to deliver a product or service were clear-cut and directly attributable to that service. In fact, if that were the case, it wouldn't exist at all. Costs that can be readily identified with a particular service using a reasonable amount of effort can be handled via the traditional accounting system. These are called the direct costs of producing a service. Since the vast majority of nonprofits produce services rather than manufactured products, we will use the term service, although the principles would be the same for product manufacturing. Some examples of direct costs might be:

- Salaries of employees delivering the service
- Their supplies
- Their equipment
- Their telephone calls
- Expenses of the physical space they use.

But what about the expense of keeping the financial records associated with the service? What about the cost of the organization's executive director or president? The legal advice the corporation receives? The sign in front of the institution's office? These are all legitimate indirect costs of doing business that must be taken into consideration in identifying a meaningful cost. If the nonprofit corporation provides only a single service, and does not conduct its own fund raising, then effectively there is no such thing as indirect costs. But as soon as it provides two or more distinct services, or conducts its own fund-raising, its management and possibly its funders will want to know the answer to the question, "How much does it cost?" and only a cost accounting system can provide the answers.

In any organization, there are two types of activities—the services the institution is in existence to provide, and those activities that support the delivery of those services. For instance, in the Campaign to Clean Up America (CCUA), such things as recycling and public education are the reasons the organization was established in the first place. Bookkeeping and marketing staff, even though they may work very closely with recycling or public education staff, exist solely to support the latter.

There is no single accepted set of names for these two categories of activity. CCUA's recycling and public education programs might be called mission centers, direct services, program centers, line programs, or the like. Bookkeeping and marketing might be called service centers, support services, or administrative services. Whatever the names, the distinction between these two types of costs

The Model Chart of Accounts Project

In matters of nonprofit financial reporting and cost accounting, what do these groups have in common: the IRS, state attorney generals, foundations, and nonprofit organizations?

Nothing, unfortunately.

Virtually all funders and regulators of nonprofit corporations require some sore of financial reporting. Over the years, in the absence of any single coordinating body, each consumer of nonprofits' financial reports has developed its own unique grouping of definitions, accounts, and reporting formats. Any overlap of design or information requested seems purely coincidental.

For their part, nonprofits struggle with this lack of standardization every time they complete a fiscal year and must send a different report to as many places as they have funders. More important, the explosion of forms and formats prevents any real comparative analysis across the field.

An enterprising researcher wants to change all that. Bill Levis, project manager for the Nonprofit Quality Reporting Project at New York's Baruch College/CUNY and his colleagues have developed a Model Chart of Accounts (MCOA) for nonprofits of all kinds. The group's key insight is that nonprofit financial reporting does not have to be such a hodgepodge, and that many parts of the sector will respond to a better idea when they see it. Levis notes that when the United Way of America published a financial accounting guide

will pop up later in significant ways. We will use the terms "program" and "support."

In keeping with our central premise that this is a book for consumers of financial information rather than producers, we will not get into the specifics of setting up and maintaining a cost accounting system. Instead, we will focus on how to evaluate an existing system or how to think about a new one.

There are two things that the average nonprofit cost accounting system has to do well if it is to provide managers with useful information: (1) distinguish between direct and indirect costs, and (2) assign certain support costs to other support costs before the entire cost of support gets divided among all direct services. (Note

(continued)

several years ago with detailed illustrative examples, many non-profits adopted it wholesale, right down to the same account coding that the manual used.

The Levis group is not asking any regulator or funding source to abandon its form. Instead, they are asking that any report-requiring body cooperate with the project by helping to crosswalk their chart of accounts with that of the MCOA. That way, nonprofits can enter their data once and produce reports coded to specific report users' demands.

The MCOA argument is that it will improve the quality of reports that funding sources receive while reducing the cost and burden of those reports to the nonprofit. They are especially interested in working with software suppliers and auditors to accomplish these objectives. Levis and his colleagues say they also plan to work with nonprofit accounting software vendors to help accomplish this task.

Ultimately, the goal is to standardize the nonprofit world's financial reporting terminology, definitions, and practices. If many different parties adopt the idea, it will be possible to produce meaningful surveys and data analysis. While that goal may be appropriately ambitious, it is perfectly reasonable to expect that a well conceived plan will help diminish some of the unnecessary confusion and communication problems in this field.

that this is for internal management purposes only since the AICPA guides and the IRS form 990 instructions do not permit it for external reporting.)

INDIRECT COSTS

In most instances, the difference between direct and indirect costs is easily handled by the accounting system. In fact, if the accounting system is unable to identify indirect costs, take it as a wake-up call to find out what's wrong. The real issue with indirect costs is how they are defined. For reasons which we will discuss later, indirect costs are inherently slippery characters. No one seems to define them in exactly the same way, unless they are operating in a very tightly regulated environment.

Worse, indirect costs seem to be morally suspect. Not thirty minutes before these words were written there appeared on local radio an advertisement for a charity golf tournament whose chief fund-raising appeal was that all money raised would go directly to services with no allowance for administration, a classic form of indirect cost. Admirable as these sentiments are, they ignore the reality that it takes administrative—indirect—effort simply to receive donated dollars. Moreover, refusing to pay any share of administrative costs with one's donated dollars only means that others will have to pay more than their share.

The effect of this free-form definition of indirect costs is that comparisons among many types of nonprofit organizations are pointless. Unless the chart of accounts (see Box on pages 74–75) and related procedures for two organizations are extremely similar, comparing indirect costs will be misleading at best and counter-productive at worst. Nevertheless, comparisons for internal purposes can still be valuable and are the basis for calculating actual costs of providing services.

CERTAIN SUPPORT COSTS GET ASSIGNED TO OTHER SUPPORT COSTS

If the cost accounting system can distinguish between direct and indirect costs, it passes its first test. Next comes the hard part. Some indirect costs are rightfully borne by both program services and support services. For example, occupancy costs such as heat, lights, and air conditioning must be carried by all types of services whether they are engaged in providing program services directly or supporting them. The principle is that each type of support service that makes use of another support service must take on its share of that support service before being broken up and distributed across the program services. Exhibit 6.1 shows a brief example of how this might work for CCUA.

The structure of this analysis bears explaining. The ultimate goal is to get a number under the total cost column that is the sum of the total direct costs of each program plus all of the support costs shown on the lines to the right. In effect, as the total direct cost for each program marches to the right, it passes through each column of support costs, where it picks up its fair share of those costs. The sum of all these direct costs and pieces of support costs then gets divided by the number of units of service the program has delivered to arrive at what can be called the "fully loaded" cost. More on each of these elements later.

There is an underlying logic here that is important to note. The columns are arrayed in a very specific order, starting with those support costs that affect the greatest number of other service centers and support costs. For CCUA, the first support cost to be distributed is the cost of management and general activities. All direct services take management resources, but so do support activities such as fund-raising. The result is that every type of activity must carry its share.

Fund-raising is next because it affects all other departments except management. Notice that the sum of fund-raising costs has increased from $103,500 in the original budget to $118,735 in this analysis because fund-raising was just assigned its share of management resources of $15,235. This newly swelled fund-raising cost then gets broken down according to some reasonable basis for allocation among the three direct service programs. In this example, we have assumed that the rough size of each program's expenses is a reasonable guide to allocating management and general costs. The result is a "fully loaded" cost because each direct cost has picked up its share of the load of each type of support service.

Deciding how to allocate portions of costs is always tricky. Sometimes there is an obvious basis, such as using cost per square foot to allocate occupancy expenses. Even with such a straightforward basis, however, there may be complications. For example, it may be theoretically easy enough to measure the square footage used by each department, but common areas such as halls and stairways and the copy machine alcove must also be factored into the equation.

Percentage of payroll is a popular basis for allocation, the theory being that the demands on management and general resources can be expected to roughly parallel the percentage of total staff a particular program uses. This may be generally true, but when it fails as a standard, it fails miserably. For instance, setting up a new

Expense or Program Category	Total Costs	Management & General	Fund-Raising
Management and general	130,800		
Fund-Raising	103,500	15,235	
Volunteer teams	252,900	37,226	38,247
Public education/ seminars	156,600	23,051	23,683
Recycling	375,600	55,288	56,804
TOTALS	1,019,400	130,800	118,734

Exhibit 6.1 Allocation of Costs

Total Cost	Total Units of Service	Full Cost	
328,373	11 Teams	29,852	Per Team
203,335	32 Seminars	6,354	Per Seminar
487,692	1500 Days	325	Per Day
1,019,400			
			0

Exhibit 6.1 Continued

program typically demands extraordinary management resources yet rarely provides additional reimbursement for those expenses. Or programs may use a disproportionately high number of staff but prove to be relatively easy to run, while smaller programs may necessarily require much administrative support. Using the program's total revenue as a percentage of the nonprofit's total revenue may also be an acceptable method for allocating costs, but this choice is susceptible to the same pitfalls as payroll percentages. For CCUA, we relied on percentages of the total spending amounts in question rather than any more complicated basis such as personnel hours. Parenthetically, actual time reporting is often the best source of guidance about how to charge time, and for staff exempt from federal fair labor standards, this can be accomplished as easily as using time studies done randomly throughout the year.

Visually and mathematically, this cost analysis has a distinguishing characteristic. Each of the two columns being allocated starts at a point one line lower than the previous column. In a larger organization with a more complicated cost analysis, the series of downward steps might stretch clear across the page, looking very much like a neat set of stairs. This is why Exhibit 6.1 symbolizes the essence of what is called a *stepdown analysis*. Each column picks up its share of costs from the one to its left, then steps itself down to the remaining columns to its right until all indirect costs have been allocated.

This exhibit is nothing more than one version of a cost analysis for one organization. Different organizations will chose different methods for entirely different and valid reasons. Whatever the method chosen, it should meet four criteria (see Box). First, it should be consistently applied across the entire organization and

---

The Four Tests of a Cost Allocation System

- Consistently applied over time
- Reasonable choice of allocation bases
- Flexible and practical
- Conforms to applicable industry standards.

over a period of time. Second, it should be a reasonable method of allocation, meaning that it should not use tortured logic simply to support a predetermined outcome. Third, it should be flexible in the sense that it should fit all programs' cost accounting needs without significant reworking just to arrive at a fully loaded cost figure. Finally, it should conform to prevailing standards for the particular field of nonprofit endeavor, if any.

Readers with a fondness for simplicity will ask why we do not simply allocate a share of fund-raising costs and a share of management and general costs to each of CCUA's programs rather than go through this exercise. The answer is that we could, if we were willing to accept a less precise calculation of costs. Managers make that kind of calculation frequently for rough planning purposes, but if one is going to go through the effort of analyzing costs, it makes sense to get them as precise as possible.

A brief digression to highlight the obvious: CCUA needs a cost accounting analysis because it offers different types of services. If it were a single service nonprofit, there would be little point in analyzing costs since a few simple divisions as just described would be enough to get a cost per unit of service. What this cost analysis does is to differentiate the three types of service and load each one with the appropriate mix of indirect costs. Even if CCUA were a single service organization with several different departments or program units delivering the service, it would require this kind of cost accounting.

Be aware that Exhibit 6.1 is a completely backward-looking exercise. The fiscal year is over, the expenses have accumulated, and all we are doing here is putting these well-behaved figures in their proper columns. There is an implied orderliness in these calculations that simply is not real. To give the cost accounting some punch, one might go back, say, three years in order to see how costs behaved over time and to draw at least some tentative inferences about how they will behave in the future.

ANOTHER USE FOR COST DATA

The practical usefulness of knowing a nonprofit's true costs cannot be underestimated for planning purposes. Building next year's budget or evaluating a potential new program is much easier with

good cost information. Especially when considering a new program, there are multiple uncertainties. How many units of service
should we plan to deliver? At what price? How will we know if the
new program is financially healthy? Is there a financial point below
which we should consider terminating it? These questions can all
be answered by using the output of a cost accounting system.

The classic form of cost planning is called *breakeven analysis.*
Done properly, breakeven analysis can give practicing managers
a simple yet powerful tool for estimating the impact of new ventures. Breakeven analysis starts with the presumption that there
are two types of costs in any organization: (1) those that stay fixed
regardless of what happens to the program, and (2) those that vary
according to the volume of service the program delivers.

Fixed costs are easy to understand and relatively easy to identify. They are the expenses of "opening the doors," the costs that
one must incur just to be prepared to provide the service regardless of whether one actually delivers one unit of service or a thousand. Typically, fixed costs are considered in the context of a
particular service or program, so that in CCUA's recycling program some fixed costs would be equipment rental agreements, occupancy costs, and depreciation for whatever assets the program
is assigned. Each of these costs is inescapable if CCUA wants to
run a recycling program. The organization must expect to spend
that money no matter what kind of revenue the program produces.

Other costs will vary with the volume of service provided and
therefore are called *variable costs.* Many of the other expenses fall
into this category. For example, the cost of supplies can be presumed to increase in roughly direct relationship to the amount of
service delivered.

Unfortunately, many other costs are not so neatly categorized
because a part of them is fixed and another part is variable.
Salaries and wages are a good example of this type of expense,
since a certain number of positions can be expected to be necessary just to open the doors, but an increase in volume will neces-
sitate additional staff. A recycling program will need at least a
telephone line or two, the installation charge and basic service for
which is assumed as part of a contract and consequently is fixed.
But the rest of the telephone bill will be for usage, and that presumably will go up or down in an approximate relationship to
volume.

These other costs are called semi-fixed or semi-variable, depending on which is their dominant character. One way to think about them so as to allow them to co-exist with the concept of fixed costs is to regard them as variable (or fixed) *within a certain range of volume.* Over the long run, all costs are variable because whatever gives them their fixed nature is usually only true for a defined period of time. Occupancy costs, which seem fixed for the moment, will change once the rental agreement is renegotiated or when the program changes in size so much that it needs new quarters. Depreciation is fixed for a year at a time, but even that will go up should new assets be acquired that need to be depreciated. With this understanding, we can proceed to the fundamental breakeven formula:

Breakeven volume = Fixed costs + (Variable costs × Units served)

The same idea in traditional formula format looks like this:

$$B = F + (V)(U)$$

Where B = Breakeven
F = Fixed costs
V = Variable costs, expressed per unit of service
U = Number of units served

For example, if a child care program knew its fixed costs for an after-school program were $32,000 and its variable cost was $1,100 per child, its breakeven point for a 100-child program would be:

$$\$142,000 = 32,000 + (1,100)(100)$$

Revenues of less than $142,000 would be inadequate to cover the program's costs; conversely, revenues over this point would result in a surplus.

Practically, breakeven analysis is more often used to determine the desired level of utilization, or the number of children in this case. It can also be very helpful in determining an appropriate price level in those cases where the nonprofit is free to set its own prices. Leaving any one variable unassigned to a value and then performing elementary algebra will yield the recommended amount for that quantity.

COST ACCOUNTING VS. COST REPORTING

A final word about the difference between cost accounting and cost reporting. Cost accounting is almost purely a management exercise, while cost reporting brings the nonprofit into areas with legal and contractual implications. One must have at least a basic cost accounting system in order to report costs accurately to an external party such as a funder. However, the cost reporting function is often so structured and carefully laid out that the pressure is on the financial person to master the reporting system rather than produce anything of value to management. That is why a nonprofit operating in a heavily regulated cost-based field will still need a separate cost accounting system in order to make informed decisions.

Even a modest cost accounting system can offer the nonprofit manager a powerful tool for managing programs. For any given period, it can reveal the underlying economics of programs in as much detail as desired. It can show, in a standardized fashion, which services are financially viable and which are not. As a planning tool, it can help suggest which service directions are most promising and which should be deferred. Without exaggeration, it is probably the single most potent analytical tool the average manager can use for decision making.

Which is why the output of a nonprofit cost accounting system may need to be ignored. Cost accounting in a for-profit organization rightfully offers more value than it does in a nonprofit setting, because a for-profit organization needs to stick with its winners and tolerate its money-losers only if they show promise of making money or at least adding value eventually. In nonprofits, the crucial measure is whether a program supports the mission and not solely whether it has a positive bottom line. Sometimes carrying a money-losing program is simply the right thing to do, and that alone is a legitimate reason for keeping it.

Cost accounting can be useful even when it delivers bad news about a losing program. For one thing, it will document that the program's economics are out of sync and that alone may be enough to tease some additional dollars out of a funding source. For another, managers are always better off knowing the precise location and reason for a problem rather than having to guess about it. Finally, a cost accounting system can help identify other programs better able to subsidize the occasional money-loser through higher profits.

So the real message here is that a cost accounting program is worse than useless if it becomes the sole measuring standard for deciding whether to keep a program. Mission should rule, not the activities designed to support mission. To paraphrase Oscar Wilde only slightly, a cynic is a person who knows the cost of everything, and the value of nothing.

CHAPTER SEVEN

Auditing: Choosing and Using an Auditor

Time to rush into an area where angels fear to tread as we consider the role, selection, and use of outside auditors. Independent audits are ingenious transactions. Here you have one party, usually some type of funding source, requiring a second party, the nonprofit corporation, to hire outsiders to examine the organizational equivalent of personal possessions and then file a public report on their findings. What's more, the whole thing is an entirely private arrangement, with no direct government involvement in the actual inspection.

Read the opinion letter in Exhibit 7.1 carefully. It says exactly what it means, not surprisingly, since the conventional wording has been tested and revised continuously for many years. The auditor says that he or she has inspected the books and records and found them to be adequate enough to generate the financial statements that are attached to it. More important, the auditor says explicitly that those financial statements convey reliable information.

Most practicing managers, on the whole, would rather not have external audits. They take up valuable staff time, disrupt operations for anywhere from a few days to several months, cost money, and can produce surprises. Sure, they can and should provide some valuable suggestions for improving things, and the process can even help shape an organization's future. But few managers would voluntarily submit to an audit once every year solely on the basis of these benefits.

We have audited the accompanying balance sheet of _____
as of June 30, 199X, and the related statements of support, revenues and
expenses and changes in fund balances and of functional expenses for
the year then ended. These financial statements are the responsibility of
the management of _____. Our responsibility is to express
an opinion on these financial statements based on our audit.

We conducted our audit in accordance with generally accepted auditing standards and *Government Auditing Standards* issued by the Comp-
troller General of the United States. Those standards require that we
plan and perform the audit to obtain reasonable assurance about
whether the financial statements are free of material misstatement. An
audit includes examining, on a test basis, evidence supporting the
amounts and disclosures in the financial statements. An audit also includes assessing the accounting principles used and significant estimates made by management, as well as evaluating the overall financial
statement presentation. We believe that our audit provides a reasonable
basis for our opinion.

In our opinion, the 199X financial statements referred to above present
fairly, in all material respects, the financial position of _____
at June 30, 199X, and the results of its operations and changes in fund
balances for the year then ended in conformity with generally accepted
accounting principles.

September 22, 199X

Exhibit 7.1   Sample Independent Auditors' Opinion Letter

The audience for that letter, then, is outside the nonprofit organization. Presumably, management already knows that their
financial systems and practices produce reliable information, but
who is really going to believe them? Too many opportunities to
do a little self-promotion might obscure the real financial condition of the organization. Outside third-party observers without
the same self-interested incentives can be trusted more.

Why would those other than management care about internal financial matters anyway? The answer is the same for both nonprofits and for-profits: money. In one form or another, suppliers of
funds have the most influence over whether and how auditors do
their work. In the for-profit environment, those suppliers are

banks, investors, and stockholders. Nonprofits' equivalents are banks, foundations, donors, and the government as a purchaser of goods and services. Each interest-holder has a different motive for wanting reassurance about financial conditions.

AUDIT, REVIEW, AND COMPILATION

The practice of outside accountants looking at an entity's financial records has coalesced into three distinct levels: audit, review, and compilation. Each type of report offers a different mix of complexity of the analysis, time required for its completion, and strength of assurance given (Exhibit 7.2).

A compilation is the lowest end of the continuum, involving little more than the gathering together of various financial records into a standardized, readable format. The accountant expresses no opinions on the material presented and does no tests to confirm its veracity.

A review goes one step beyond a simple compilation. In a review, the accountant compiles the information into standardized formats and then performs some quick analyses to see if it seems to have internal consistency. The accountant offers no opinion, only what is called "negative assurance": "I'm not aware of anything that would materially alter these statements." The report reader gets information presented in traditional formatting in addition to the comfort of knowing that an intelligent set of eyes has reviewed the material for extreme inconsistencies or significant gaps in data.

The audit is the deepest, most intensive examination of a set of books possible. Auditors test management's representations in many different ways according to pre-established protocols. In

Compilation	Review	Audit
Low		High

Degree of: Complexity
Time Required
Assurance

Exhibit 7.2 The Three Levels of Reporting

addition, prolonged exposure to the books and records gives auditors greater opportunity to spot errors and omissions and to make suggestions for improvement.

At the same time, there are no guarantees here. Unless one second-guesses 100 percent of all transactions, there is really no basis to certify the absence of fraud or material misstatement— and even then there would need to be a lot of additional second-guessing in other areas. Instead, the audit opinion offers assurance that skilled accounting professionals have examined the financial records and feel that they can be relied upon. In short, an audit offers exactly the level of reliability that the opinion letter says it does.

Who Uses What

Because the market for auditing services is driven by who wants the assurance, different types and sizes of organizations need different types of work. Compilations tend to be favored by small, relatively unsophisticated private for-profit companies. For a variety of reasons, they are not an option for most nonprofits. Reviews are an alternative to a full audit for certain nonprofit corporations, although state laws may make this choice available only to groups with the smallest revenues. By contrast, reviews are a popular choice for many privately held for-profit businesses since they give some minimal level of outside evaluation at a lower price and with less disclosure than an audit.

Whenever maximum accountability is required, managers must choose a traditional audit. This is why most of the larger nonprofit public charities will be audited. In a sense, the various governmental and other regulations stipulating audit types are just affirming what a prudent public charity manager would do anyway. The public's trust in a charity is so fragile and yet so critical to its functioning that independent audits are a natural means of gaining that assurance.

The Audit Equation

There is a dynamic at work in nonprofit audits that rarely gets spoken of directly between the organization and its auditors. We call it the audit equation, and it is the balance between auditing

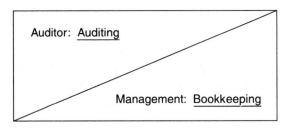

Exhibit 7.3 The Audit Equation

and bookkeeping shown in Exhibit 7.3. The former is the auditors' job, the latter is the responsibility of management. If both parties labor quietly at their respective chores with little effective communication between them about this central expectation, the result can be a mutual misunderstanding or even a breakdown in the relationship. Remember that the audit is supposed to be an opinion on the reliability of *management's* financial statements. That means that management is expected to prepare the statements, and the outside auditors will analyze them and the systems that produced the information so as to offer an opinion on their collective reliability. When management fails to do things like reconcile bank statements, prepare depreciation schedules, and even enter basic accounting data, the auditors have to do it instead.

When the outside auditors have to do this type of work, it increases the audit cost for the organization since the auditors must also act as bookkeepers. More important, if it happens to a significant extent, the auditors find themselves effectively auditing their own work. This impairs their independence and in extreme cases can even prevent the issuance of an opinion.

The simple way to avoid these problems is to keep the audit equation in mind. Management must be careful always to do all operations in its corner, leaving the auditors to concentrate on their corner. The disk accompanying this book gives an audit self-test for clarifying this question.

THE AUDITOR MARKET

Like all other professions, auditing services have their own distinct and definable market. Individual Certified Public Accountants

(CPAs) are the professionals qualified and licensed to give an opinion about the financial health of business entities. They exist in many different forms, from the part-timer who works out of a spare bedroom to the sole practitioner employing a dozen or more staff, to one of many professional personnel in an international firm. These professionals can be found on just about any type of engagement, from nonprofits to start up proprietary businesses to individuals.

Each type of audit firm tends to shape its clientele in predictable ways. Small firms and sole practitioners, as might be expected, handle small local audits and reviews. When an organization grows too large or too sophisticated for this level, or needs consulting services, it will often gravitate to smaller national or large regional firms where it can find more nonprofit specialists and access to the latest industry knowledge. Massive national public charities often use one of the Big Six, the nickname for the six largest auditing firms.

Elements of Auditor Choice

Most nonprofit managers regard the yearly financial audit as a commodity. There is intense debate over this point among auditors themselves, but in economic terms if most buyers see something as a commodity, that's the way the market will behave. What truly distinguishes one audit from another is when it is carried out by auditors with deep knowledge of the industry they are auditing. Even if the results are the same, the audit done by industry experts is far more likely to go smoothly and quickly and to teach management a thing or two in the process. Research shows that one of the prime reasons for making an auditor change is industry familiarity, and auditing firms with marketing savvy are beginning to organize themselves to offer that feature to the industries in which they specialize.

Who chooses the auditor? In truth, this is one of those instances where the textbooks say one thing and real world practice says another. For the record, the board should make the decision. Further, the board should meet with its auditors at least once a year to get a firsthand account of the agency's financial status, and it ought to maintain at least an informal dialogue in the interim.

In reality, some boards are either too busy, too uninterested, or too intimidated to take the lead in an auditing relationship. It then falls to the executive director to make the choice and carry out the process. By itself, there's nothing fatal about this scenario. It just means that the agency's fiduciaries have voluntarily given up a means of insuring accountability. When this single step is part of a larger pattern of refusing to demand accountability from management, it can mean that an important element of leadership is lacking.

Whoever makes it, the choice of an auditor involves balancing a variety of factors (see Box). No choice is likely to be perfect, nor is a satisfactory fit guaranteed to stay that way indefinitely. Still, there are many identifiable aspects of auditor choice and at least one or two are probably going to be the major points of consideration. Here are some of them:

- *Industry Knowledge.* Industry knowledge is a hard-won commodity that an audit firm acquires either by hiring people from the industry, merging with firms that have the expertise, or by cultivating the knowledge among its own professionals over a period of time. No matter how it gets done it represents a major investment of time, money, and energy. For this reason, there are usually only a few audit firms in any given industry with substantive expertise.

  This tendency is strongly reinforced when the financial stakes are high or when some element of the industry involves complex financial transactions. When either of these things is true, the number of audit firms with true industry expertise is likely to be counted on the fingers of one hand. Often one or two firms will dominate, at least regionally, and the rest of the load will be carried by a handful of secondary players.

  The spread of audit firms also tends to reflect the relative age of the industry and its degree of maturity. Generally speaking, the older the nonprofit's field, the more concentrated will be the number of firms with expertise. Conversely, the newer fields will tend to display a wide range of auditor choice. Universities, for instance, are usually served by only a handful of firms, while AIDS projects are so new and so rapidly evolving that there are probably as many auditors as

How to Purchase Audit Services

Auditing services are professional services. Once a minimum level of technical competence is established, the primary goal of a professional services procurement is to determine the fit between the professional service provider and the service user. Resist the urge to demand responses with fine-point specificity, as though the answers were going to be placed side-by-side on a spreadsheet for comparison. That's how you buy wheat, apples, milk, and other commodities, not professional services.

The traditional way to solicit auditing services is through a Request for Proposals (RFP). There is no single correct way to design an RFP, but here are some things to keep in mind:

• *Describe the organization thoroughly.* What is your mission? When were you founded? Are you a 501(C)(3) or some other type of nonprofit? What are your services? Are there special circumstances the auditors should know about (for example, this is the first financial audit after a merger)? It is not necessary to include a copy of audited financial statements at this stage—you can make them available during pre-proposal interviews—but do include summary financial information such as revenues and their sources and balance sheet data.

• *State what you need.* State explicitly what you need the auditing firm to do. Some nonprofits want their auditors to audit the financial

there are agencies to be audited. As the field stabilizes and matures, so will the auditor complement serving it.

• *Price.* Wherever industry knowledge is unimportant to large numbers of audit clients, competition will almost always be on price. The best way to get a low price is to find a sole practitioner or very small local firm that wants to get into the nonprofit field. Not only does a sole practitioner have lower overhead than an established firm, but he or she may be willing to discount deeply just to get the business. Such bargain-basement tactics could also backfire if the auditor discovers

(continued)

statements, complete the tax return(s), and file various financial reports, while others want only the audited financials.

• *Request qualifications.* Request that the auditors describe their qualifications to audit your organization. Explicitly link your needs with their qualifications, such as "Must have experience performing OMB A-133 audits."

• *Describe your timetable, decision process and selection criteria.* Detail how you will make a decision, when, and on what basis. A formula with points for various criteria is bureaucratic but probably harmless. Best to be straightforward here. *Note:* By all rights, the auditors report to the board, so they should be the ultimate decision makers even if staff does most of the work.

As much as possible, send the RFP to practitioners and firms you know to be skilled in your industry and appropriate providers of service. Be prepared to meet with each candidate in person (if they don't request a personal visit, ask yourself why). Give plenty of time for all parties concerned to do their jobs—four to eight weeks should work—and plan to put in at least as much time managing the process as any single candidate will in responding to you. Use the process as a management tool.

The accompanying computer disk contains a sample RFP.

that the job is much more demanding than expected or if it requires greater skill and knowledge than the individual possesses.

In the end, audit pricing is susceptible to exactly the same forces that drive other professional services. The field is large enough and the choice of potential auditors wide enough that just about every nonprofit should be able to find fee level.

• *Name Recognition.* Financial audits aren't in the same class as luxury automobiles, but some of the same intangible considerations apply anyway. Certain auditing firms have better name recognition than others, conferring a kind of prestige on their clients solely by virtue of having been hired by them. That kind of effect is often associated with a national firm or a large local practice. Few people involved in an audit decision want to publicly acknowledge this factor, however, so it may go entirely unmentioned during the process of choosing an auditor. In fact, it may never surface at all.

- *Staff Continuity.* Auditing staff turn over as much or if not more than other professionals. Traditionally, accounting firms are organized as pyramids with staff at the bottom, managers in the middle and partners at the top. In this arrangement, employees enter at the bottom and work their way to the top. The odds against their ever reaching that peak—should they even desire it—are high. In some larger firms, fewer than one of every 25 new employees eventually makes the partner level. As a result, planned terminations are built into the process.

  When staff accountants and managers leave it can cause disruption on both sides of the client-auditor relationship. The audited nonprofit must get to know replacement staff, there may be duplication of effort, and there is the constant specter of the replacement staff themselves eventually leaving. In this common dynamic, the reliable source of continuity should be the partners of the firm, or perhaps the senior managers.

  For some nonprofits, partner continuity is not enough. Either for the practical reasons mentioned above or for psychological ones, the nonprofit feels strongly that it must have the same audit team year after year. In that case, the solution is simple and identical to the pricing dilemma resolution described earlier—go for the sole practitioner or the very smallest firm. The internal pressure to move up or out will not exist in the smallest firms, and many small firms will opt for longevity over almost anything else if given the choice. Again, however, this almost certainly means steep tradeoffs in industry knowledge, but it can mean increased continuity if done properly.

  Insistence on auditor staff continuity can be a sign of middle management insecurity or worse. Having the same personnel audit the organization year after year makes the process more predictable and comfortable, but in truth comfort and predictability are low on the list of audit objectives. After all, a fresh outside perspective is at the heart of an audit. In many high stakes situations, firms will actually rotate partners and other staff after a set period of time just to take advantage of new eyes.

- *Audit Firm Size and Geography.* There is a natural tendency for organizations of all types to gravitate toward service suppliers of their own size. Partly this is the result of economics—big companies need services delivered by suppliers who can cope with other big companies—but partly it is stylistic as well. The local nonprofit community development corporation may strongly prefer local merchants as part of its commitment to the community. The huge university may choose its copier paper supplier through an impersonal request-for-proposal process and not care where they are located as long as they can provide the product. So it is with the choice of auditors. A large regional nonprofit may choose a small national or regional audit firm for its credibility. A small nonprofit may simply go across the street.

  Geography is not as important from the audit firm's perspective as it frequently is from the nonprofit's. Nonprofit staff may feel the need to have ready access to the auditors during potentially difficult situations such as accounting system installations or conversions, but for the most part distance is not a major factor in accomplishing the technical part of the audit work.

GETTING VALUE FROM THE AUDIT

The Management Letter

At the end of the audit process the audit team has accumulated a tremendous amount of knowledge, new or updated, about how the nonprofit runs its affairs. The team will put some of that information into its final report, but a good measure of it will never see the inside of a financial statement and yet is extremely valuable to management. The solution to this dilemma is the management letter.

The point to remember about a management letter is simple—
get one. You deserve it. You and your staff put in the time, you
worked through the entire audit process, and now it's payback
time. The hours that these informed outsiders spent looking at the
nonprofit from the inside out can produce valuable insights about
what areas need improvement. The letter should include both findings and recommendations for action, so it's like the first step of a
how-to course. Take advantage of it.

Specialized Reporting

In recent years, the federal government has become increasingly
active in stipulating auditing requirements for groups receiving
federal funding of any sort. As a result, very specific audit guidelines now exist for universities, hospitals, governmental entities,
and public charities receiving direct or, in some cases, indirect federal funds. In addition, professional standard-setting societies in
the accounting field have established standards for auditing and
for the training of personnel who work on these types of audits.

Some of these requirements include Office of Management and
Budget Circular A-133 (OMB A-133), the Single Audit Act, the
Guide to Audits of Nonprofit and Governmental Entities (the "Yel-
low Book"), and various pronouncements of the Financial Ac-
counting Standards Board and the Governmental Accounting
Standards Board.

These governmental requirements tend to shift more of the burden for examining recipients of federal funds from the government
itself to private auditors. For example, OMB A-133 dictates a series of signed opinion letters from the auditors on matters ranging
from the effectiveness of the internal controls governing federal
funds to compliance with certain federal laws. In a different time
and place, this type of certification would very likely have been
done by the government itself. Today, government requires that the
private sector do it.

This trend has had two effects, both of which should be noted
by nonprofit managers. The first is that the agency's own auditors
have turned at least partially into government-mandated watch-
dogs. This can chill the relationship with a nonprofit, especially if
neither party acknowledges the impact that all of these additional
requirements impose. The second effect is that governmental and

nonprofit auditing is becoming more standardized and a bit more technical. This raises the hurdle for auditors wishing to get into the field or stay in it. For instance, there are now minimum continuing education requirements for those who work on these types of audits.

The implication is that it is no longer practical for small to medium size firms to do just one or two such audits since they will have to invest a minimum amount of time in learning the rules and staying current. In turn, this will cause firms to pull out of incidental nonprofit auditing relationships or to make a larger specialization of it. At present, the nonprofit auditor market is fragmented. In part this is because nonprofits tend to be smaller organizations more likely to come to the attention of small, local audit practices. This is an industry practically begging for consolidation, so as average agency size and complexity increase, the total numbers of audit firms active in the field will decrease.

One can see the same patterns at work in varying degrees across the nonprofit field. Universities, for example, are now so large and complex that relatively few audit practices are able even to consider taking one on as a client, whereas battered women's shelters are so small and diverse that it is highly unlikely that there will be a concentration of audit talent in a few firms. As the government's demands on auditors rise, and as the various categories of nonprofits themselves mature, the potential number of nonprofit auditors will decline. This diminished choice should be offset somewhat as the quality of services provided by those who do choose to specialize in the field increases, meaning an overall increase in value for consumers.

CONCLUSION

Yearly financial audits are a necessary part of nonprofit financial management. The motivation for outside inspection in this field has more to do with accountability than the protection of investment characteristic of the for-profit world. Still, the process holds the potential of great usefulness to managers if it is handled effectively. All it takes is a little bit of time, skill, and knowledge of the industry to make it a mini-asset of the nonprofit corporation.

PART THREE

Operations

CHAPTER EIGHT

Cash Flow Management: Why Cash Is King

Cash is king in the nonprofit realm as elsewhere. Those who have it can do just about anything. Those who do not, stagger. Adequate cash allows the organization to pay its bills. More than adequate cash gives the organization a source of additional revenue, an operating cushion, and liberation from some of the daily grind of financial existence. Much more than adequate cash confers something more: power.

Some of the most powerful of all nonprofit institutions are hospitals and universities. The major versions of each almost always have a solid cash position, derived from a number of sources, which they can use either in operations or investments. Their power comes with their control of capital, and controlling a sizable portion of cash means controlling some potent capital. (For more on the role of capital in a nonprofit organization, see Chapter Nine on capital structure.)

Nonprofit organizations with adequate cash can do two critical things: Survive crises and take advantage of opportunities. Few crises are true threats to an organization's existence—even if it may seem that way at the time—as long as the group has the resources to respond. It takes more than cash, of course, but cash can make an effective response immeasurably easier. Similarly, it takes cash to buy a building, start up a program, or do some research, and all of these things can be an "investment" in the nonprofit's future. Organizations with inadequate cash are shut off from those potential investments and easily trapped by crises.

The need to manage cash flow is particularly acute in a nonprofit setting because few nonprofits operate as cash businesses.

Not only is this inherent in the services—as distinct from, say, a bar or a pizza shop—but funders like the accountability that it brings. And, naturally, no nonprofit is immune from the effects of forces as diverse as economic swings, abrupt changes in market conditions, or natural disasters.

The job of managing cash flow consists of creating cash or moving assets toward a liquid, or cash state, and incurring the right liabilities. The trick is knowing when and how to do this.

UP THE BALANCE SHEET

The simplest way to "create" cash is to change an asset from a less liquid form to cash. Think of the different classes of assets as being like the different states of water. Down at the bottom of the asset side you'll find land, buildings, and equipment—very tangible assets. These are like ice. They're cold, stiff, unchanging, and not responsive. Toward the middle of the continuum are things like stocks and bonds. These assets are a lot like water—they'll move when you arrange for it to happen, but left on their own they'll just puddle. At the top is cash, which is like steam—fast moving, constantly changing, and quickly disappearing.

To keep the metaphor going, part of the job of cash management consists of knowing when and where to apply a little heat to the assets. Running out of steam? Heat up some water/investments. No assets in this category? Turn to the ice.

Let's look at the example in Exhibit 8.1. Suppose that the organization represented here had yearly expenses of $3.5 million. With those kind of numbers, the balance sheet shows a pretty skimpy cash total. Ignoring the effects of depreciation (which we don't know), they need a little less than $9,600 per day to survive ($3,500,000/365 days). At this rate, they have less than two days in their cash account as shown on line 45 ($16,190/9,600).

If this manager needed cash, the first stop would be to turn the heat up under line 46, savings and temporary cash investments. There are more than ten days of cash here ($102,929/9,600). That will help a great deal, and it shouldn't be much of a problem to pull the cash from its temporary investment state. If management is smart, they will have parked those savings in the same bank where they keep their cash, so in all likelihood a phone call will do it.

Form 990 (1993)

Part IV   Balance Sheets

Note: *Where required, attached schedules and amounts within the description column should be for end-of-year amounts only.*		(A) Beginning of year		(B) End of year
Assets				
45 Cash—non-interest-bearing		*141,462*	45	*16,190*
46 Savings and temporary cash investments		*104,674*	46	*102,929*
47a Accounts receivable	47a			
b Less: allowance for doubtful accounts	47b	*339,753*	47c	*376,205*
48a Pledges receivable	48a *41,515*			
b Less: allowance for doubtful accounts	48b *16,500*	*47,401*	48c	*25,015*
49 Grants receivable		*23,858*	49	
50 Receivables due from officers, directors, trustees, and key employees (attach schedule)			50	
51a Other notes and loans receivable (attach schedule)	51a			
b Less: allowance for doubtful accounts	51b		51c	
52 Inventories for sale or use		*381,424*	52	*502,722*
53 Prepaid expenses and deferred charges		*21,405*	53	*12,675*
54 Investments—securities (attach schedule)		*34,560*	54	*23,324*
55a Investments—land, buildings, and equipment: basis	55a			
b Less: accumulated depreciation (attach schedule)	55b		55c	
56 Investments—other (attach schedule)			56	
57a Land, buildings, and equipment: basis	57a *7,710,806*			
b Less: accumulated depreciation (attach schedule)	57b *685,719*	*1,668,665*	57c	*18,506,767*
58 Other assets (describe ▶ _____)			58	
59 **Total assets** (add lines 45 through 58) (must equal line 75)		*17,781,189*	59	*19,565,827*
Liabilities				
60 Accounts payable and accrued expenses		*344,493*	60	*779,426*
61 Grants payable			61	
62 Support and revenue designated for future periods (attach schedule)			62	
63 Loans from officers, directors, trustees, and key employees (attach schedule)			63	
64a Tax-exempt bond liabilities (attach schedule)		*5,096,648*	64a	*7,311,327*
b Mortgages and other notes payable (attach schedule)			64b	
65 Other liabilities (describe ▶ _____)		*1,525,178*	65	*1,531,164*
66 **Total liabilities** (add lines 60 through 65)		*6,966,319*	66	*9,621,917*
Fund Balances or Net Assets				
Organizations that use fund accounting, check here ▶ ☐ and complete lines 67 through 70 and lines 74 and 75 (see instructions).				
67a Current unrestricted fund		*10,123,969*	67a	*9,942,855*
b Current restricted fund			67b	
68 Land, buildings, and equipment fund		*690,901*	68	*1,055*
69 Endowment fund			69	
70 Other funds (describe ▶ _____)			70	
Organizations that do not use fund accounting, check here ▶ ☐ and complete lines 71 through 75 (see instructions).				
71 Capital stock or trust principal			71	
72 Paid-in or capital surplus			72	
73 Retained earnings or accumulated income			73	
74 **Total fund balances or net assets** (add lines 67a through 70 OR lines 71 through 73; column (A) must equal line 19 and column (B) must equal line 21)		*10,814,870*	74	*9,943,910*
75 **Total liabilities and fund balances/net assets** (add lines 66 and 74)		*17,781,189*	75	*19,565,827*

Form 990 is available for public inspection and, for some people, serves as the primary or sole source of information about a particular organization. How the public perceives an organization in such cases may be determined by the information presented on its return. Therefore, please make sure the return is complete and accurate and fully describes the organization's programs and accomplishments.

Exhibit 8.1 Example of cash management

Next Stop, A/R

Still, twelve days' cash isn't a lot, they will almost certainly need more. Next stop on the continuum is usually the most promising of all, accounts receivable. This enduring reservoir of money owed to the corporation offers a lot to cash-hungry managers with the right approach.

Begin with the fact that quantifying accounts receivable is more art than science. If it were possible to peer deeply into the anatomy of this line, you would see, depending on the size and nature of the organization, hundreds or even thousands of individual transactions in varying stages of completion.

Some are simply taking a bit longer to process (and thus turn into cash) than average. Some are stretching a bit, perhaps because the person owing the money sent the check to the wrong address or has temporarily forgotten about the debt. Some are practically nonexistent and are on the verge of being ignored completely because, for whatever reason, they'll never be paid. And perhaps a few are dead beyond any doubt, don't belong here at all, and just haven't yet been removed (or "written off").

Incidentally, it's a bit troublesome that the presenters of this balance sheet feel that they will eventually collect 100 percent of their outstanding bills, a fact we can infer because they have made no allowance for doubtful accounts. If the nature of their business is such that their receivables line consists of a few big invoices due from, say, the federal government, fine. But in the absence of this type of situation, it's virtually inevitable that some amount of these accounts will never be collected, and management's estimate of how much that will be should be shown here.

To sum up—all semi-vibrant, quivering, or near death accounts traditionally get lumped into this single line as an asset of the corporation, and the manager seeking cash is well advised to look here early in the quest for cash. There are several strategies for turning accounts receivable into cash. Here are a few worth considering:

- *Prevent transactions from landing in A/R in the first place.* Once an individual bill ends up as an account receivable there's nothing preventive you can do about it. But if you can learn what put it and others like it here, maybe there are some things you can do differently next time. For example, encouraging more transactions to be done in cash up front will keep down the receivables. Simply requesting cash as payment is a start, and offering a discount for it works, too. For some nonprofits, prevention might mean checking payment sources more carefully or assigning a staff person to work with consumers to locate and verify payment sources.

- *Tell the business manager to reduce accounts receivable.* Even if you can't do anything about current accounts receivable, reducing the rate at which future accounts flow into A/R won't take long before causing a positive effect on cash flow. Without exaggeration, this one should be good for at least a 10 percent reduction in accounts receivable. What gets measured gets done, and as soon as you make it clear that you're measuring your billing department and the person responsible for it according to the number of days in receivables they report (see Chapter Four "Financial Analysis: A Few Diagnostic Tools" for a definition of days in receivables), you are almost certain to see an improvement. Make average days in receivables a component of your business manager's yearly evaluation.

Improve Invoicing Technology

Incremental progress is the theme here. Again, there's nothing to be done about accounts already languishing in A/R, but often you can find a way to tweak the billing system's technology without spending money and yet still get reduced receivables. Groups working on contract, for instance, may find that their payment source will deposit payments directly into their corporate bank account, saving a day or two in transit time. It may not seem like much, but after a while that kind of money turns into improved cash.

Borrow Against or Sell Receivables

Sometimes a bank will lend money against solid receivables. Though it doesn't happen often, this may be a way to turn line 46 into cash a bit sooner. In certain for-profit industries (the garment industry, for instance), it is commonplace to sell one's receivables to another company for a percentage less than 100 percent of expected value. The other company then chases the payments and pockets the difference between what they paid and what they collected. This is called factoring, and although there isn't any factoring in the nonprofit sector, there is a variation.

Many hospitals will sell their old receivables to such a company for a deep discount, and the company will then attempt to collect on them. At least one consultant has developed a kind of quarter-in-the-washing machine practice in which he attempts to collect old bills sent to government health insurers. He and the health care provider split the proceeds in some fashion: since he can focus exclusively on the old bills, he almost always collects something from them. By contrast, the provider's regular billing staff are highly unlikely to make good on a collection. Maintaining a billing function is a daily affair, and once a packet of bills falls off the speeding train, there is a strong temptation to leave it behind.

At the hypothetical $3.5 million volume with no depreciation cost assumed, this agency has about 39 days of cash tied up in receivables ($376,205/$9,600). On the face of it, this seems unremarkable. Without knowing more about the nonprofit's business and without some sort of standard for comparison, there is no reliable way of evaluating this record. This may already be a reasonably tight billing system with only marginal room for improvement.

Pledges Can Be Promising

Not every organization is lucky enough to have uncollected pledges sitting on its books, but these folks have $25,015 (line 48c). Two things are noteworthy here. First, this amount is after subtracting $16,500 in doubtful pledges; management apparently has greater doubts about its pledges than its bills. Second, it routinely have pledges outstanding, last year's amount totaling $47,401.

These people know how to secure and collect on pledges, and this fact gives hope for another potential source of cash. It is possible that one or more pledges could be hurried up to produce additional cash: check with the development person. It's not always possible to collect pledges early. Years ago, Princeton University received a substantial pledge from a noted financier. Fortunately for the university, they did little more than smile and say "thank you" because the pledge came from Ivan Boesky who shortly thereafter was indicted and faced more pressing demands on his time and money. In the future, the Financial Accounting Standards Board will require more pledges to be listed as receivable, after which more pledges will surely be listed as doubtful.

Other Receivables

Grants receivable (line 49) are similar to pledges receivable, although they may be slightly more collectible than pledges since they tend to come out of a formalized process rather than from individuals. In theory, receivables from insiders and other notes and loans (lines 50 and 51c) may be collectible, but for internal political reasons they're not usually worth considering.

Inventories

Four out of five readers can skip this section. They are the ones from organizations carrying no appreciable inventories (line 52) in connection with daily operations. For those that do, a single operative principle applies: Inventories can almost always be smaller than they are. Few companies, for-profit or nonprofit, are willing to state publicly that they manage their inventories well, and for good reason. Inventories of raw materials *or* finished goods (the former being more applicable here) are messy. They are hard to track, difficult to value, and prone to shrinkage. It takes great skill, better technology and lots of experience to do it well.

Valuing inventories is inherently tricky, and whole careers in accounting theory have been dedicated to the task. Real-world twists also have a pesky way of intruding. In methadone clinics, whose service is tightly regulated by the federal government, accounting conventions stipulate that the methadone inventory be listed at acquisition cost, which tends to be low. Were a clinic manager to make decisions solely on the basis of acquisition costs, he or she would miss the fact that the street value—and therefore the security risk—of a methadone inventory is many, many times the nominal price.

The one thing certain is that, accounting questions aside, *inventories cost money to acquire.* Therefore, the smaller the inventory (especially of raw goods, the most common kind in nonprofits), the less expenditure of cash required.

As with A/R, the secret is not to let transactions go into inventory in the first place. It is no accident that in the 1980s a whole school of manufacturing management, Just-In-Time (JIT), grew up around the central insight that a dollar not tied up in inventory is a dollar available for some other purpose within the organization.

Prepaid Expenses and Deferred Charges

As a source of ready cash, forget these amounts (line 53). Ever tried to get a deposit back from the telephone company? Though a current asset, this cash is iced over.

Investments

Investments in various financial instruments (lines 54–56) are unquestionably one of the most fertile sources of cash since they can usually be sold quickly. Two caveats apply: (1) dumping securities to produce cash should always be part of a planned process and not an emergency fix, and (2) it may not be as easy as it seems anyway.

In many nonprofits with large endowments held in securities, the actual instruments are under the control of a second party. Typically this second party is a professional money manager of some sort. Not only do professional money managers not want the gates to the money swinging open and shut like a screen door in a heavy breeze, but they are often under explicit instructions from the board of directors regarding transfers of funds. Getting a cash infusion in this situation is guaranteed to take some persistence.

Land, Buildings, and Equipment

Down here in the ice section of the balance sheet (line 57c) is the classic use of tangible assets for raising cash—as collateral for loans. This is one of the best reasons for adequate capitalization in a nonprofit organization, since lenders like a good base of real estate as backup for operating loans. Be aware, though, that turning tangible assets like these into cash takes time and effort. At the very least, it requires pre-arrangement with a bank. And it can also mean that the lender gets to attach strings to the use or disposal of the property for the life of the loan.

Stretch Those Payables

The simplest way to generate cash on the liability side of the balance sheet is one that everyone who manages a checkbook understands intuitively: Stretch the payables (lines 60 and 61). Or, to put it in plain English, pay bills slower. Bills the organization has accepted as legitimate but not yet paid—accounts payable—are in fact the prime source of cash for most nonprofit corporations. This is why nonprofits have a reputation for paying their bills slowly. It may be difficult to squeeze A/R or collateralize buildings, but it doesn't take much to postpone paying an invoice or delay awarding a grant.

The trick is to stretch one's payables right up to the point where it begins to cost either money or supplier goodwill. It may be easier than you would think since a surprising number of business managers and bookkeepers often seem to strive to pay all bills practically before sundown on the day they're received. Just as important, stretching the payables should be part of a coordinated, deliberate plan rather than a haphazard game of chance.

Note that our sample nonprofit has already stretched its payables to—or perhaps beyond—the breaking point. At a yearly revenue of $3,500,000, the $779,426 in payables reported here represent a hefty 22 percent of their entire year's budget. Making the reasonable assumptions that the minor share of their budget is in nonpayroll expenses and that none of the reported payables include overdue payroll, we can conclude that a huge portion of this group's nonpayroll spending is piling up in unpaid bills.

Support and Revenue Designated for Future Periods

It's nice money if you can get it. Most nonprofits have enough trouble getting revenue for the current period, let alone for the future (line 62). However, in certain situations, particularly membership organizations, it may be possible to coax some future revenue out of members ("buy a three-year membership today") fairly painlessly. Just be careful not to discount the future revenue too heavily. A dollar in three years is worth eighty or ninety cents today, not fifty cents. Done on a large scale, this kind of short-sightedness could actually hurt cash flows in the future, not help.

Loans from Officers, Directors, Trustees, and Key Employees

First question: Do you really want to be carrying these loans (line 63)? Yes it's a convenience to employees, and yes it's desirable to support officers and directors in every way possible, but consider the intangible cost. Since the early 1990s, the media has been growing more and more aware of these types of arrangements and treats them, with some justification, as the nonprofit equivalent of insider training. No, it probably isn't possible to call the loans, but not making them to begin with will ultimately save cash, not to mention public relations headaches.

Mortgages and Other Notes Payable

Any long-term debt you assume shows up here (line 64). It may seem strange at first, but activity on line 64 should be completely disconnected from cash flow management unless the terms of a line of credit cause it to be recorded here. Why? Cash flow is by definition a short-term phenomenon that should be met with short-term resources. Incurring long-term debt to take care of cash flow needs means the organization's economics are fundamentally out of sync. Translation: If you find yourself tempted to take on a mortgage to help with cash flow, regard it as a red flag.

Fund Balances (Net Assets)

Fund balances (lines 67a–74) have nothing to do with cash either, except to the extent that this accumulation of yearly surpluses will, if liabilities are held down, be offset by a greater asset base that can eventually be turned into cash if necessary.

HOW MUCH CASH IS ENOUGH?

Time now for the classic question: How much cash do we need to keep on hand? To which the only proper response is the equally classic, muddled and entirely unsatisfying: It depends.

Suppose you are starting a business, nonprofit or for-profit, and have taken care of the cash needs of all start-up costs and investments. The business is expected to do $10,000 per day every day of the year. Suppose further that this is completely a cash business. At the end of the first day, you would be $10,000 richer since no suppliers would have had to have been paid and no employees would have received a paycheck. At the end of the second day you would be nearly $20,000 ahead, minus whatever small cash outlays might have been necessary to buy emergency supplies, put gas in a vehicle, and so on. In fact, it would probably take a week or two before you had to start paying money out in the form of payroll and invoices from suppliers, but by that time you would be way ahead of things from a cash perspective—at least until the economics of your business caught up with you.

Now go in the other direction. Assume your business receives no income at all in cash, and that every dollar of revenue is received only after sending a bill for it. This would mean that you would be carrying the entire operation, paying salaries and occupancy costs and a myriad of other expenses, without an ounce of cash until you could translate your work into a bill to be sent out. Even then, you would have to continue in that cashless manner until whoever received the bill paid their money (and until that payment cleared the bank). Until that point, you get no cash in the door whatsoever.

This type of cash-flow scenario is represented by:

TOTAL DAYS ELAPSED

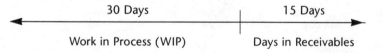

30 Days	15 Days
Work in Process (WIP)	Days in Receivables

Here, it takes 30 days to deliver the services and then bill for them. For the sake of simplicity, we've assumed that it takes no time at all to generate the bill itself; clearly an impossibility in reality, but okay for now. If the nonprofit's typical days in receivables number 15 (see Chapter Four "Financial Analysis: A Few Diagnostic Tools"), then the amount of cash needed on hand is at least 45 days worth of the agency's average expenses. To this number must be added a "cushion" to allow for slippage and unforeseen expenses.

The Fail-Safe Source of Cash—Profits

In the end, there is no better source of cash available to the non-profit corporation than profitability. Simply put, a sustained period of time in which the organization takes in more revenue than it puts out as expenses will take care of most cash flow needs quite nicely. The good thing about cash flow from operations is that it is cheap (no interest charges), readily available, and relatively easy to create. In fact, nonprofits' chronic cash shortage is partly the direct result of an industry managing itself so as to avoid profit.

There are many restrictions on a nonprofit's ability to generate a profit, some imagined and some real. Payers' rules, board of directors' (or management's) reluctance, intense demand for additional services, and simply a desire to use every last dime in the service of mission are just a few of the forces acting to keep profitability down. This means that profitability alone will enhance cash flow only slowly, probably a few percentage points a year at best. Other means will have to be used as well. Still, running a consistent profit is the best foundation for adequate cash flow.

	Jan	Feb	Mar	Apr	May
CASH IN					
Program Services	300,000	300,000	300,000	300,000	300,000
Fundraising	75,000	75,000	75,000	75,000	75,000
Miscellaneous	13,333	13,333	13,333	13,333	13,333
Total In	388,333	388,333	388,333	388,333	388,333
CASH OUT					
Salaries	252,400	252,400	252,400	252,400	252,400
Payroll Taxes	25,240	25,240	25,240	25,240	25,240
Employee Benefits	25,240	25,240	25,240	25,240	25,240
Consultants	2,500	2,500	2,500	2,500	2,500
Legal/Audit	1,250	1,250	1,250	1,250	1,250
Contracted Services	3,000	3,000	3,000	3,000	3,000
Program Supplies	45,000	45,000	45,000	45,000	45,000
Vehicle Expense	1,500	1,500	1,500	1,500	1,500
Equipment Leases	2,000	2,000	2,000	2,000	2,000
Rent	24,000	24,000	24,000	24,000	24,000
Utilities	3,000	3,000	3,000	3,000	3,000
Property Insurance	2,000	2,000	2,000	2,000	2,000
Total Out	387,130	387,130	387,130	387,130	387,130
Net Inflow (Outflow)	1,203	1,203	1,203	1,203	1,203
Beginning Balance	10,000	11,203	12,406	13,609	14,812
Ending Balance	11,203	12,406	13,609	14,812	16,015

Exhibit 8.2 Three-Zero Cash Flow Projection

The Cash Flow Projection

Now, turn to the mechanics of cash flow management. A single sheet of paper should do it, from a management perspective anyway. The cash flow projection is the heart of cash flow management, and every nonprofit corporation should use it regularly. It is and must remain strictly an internal report—not the kind of thing even the board of directors needs or should want to see routinely. Someone in the business office needs to produce the projection at least quarterly, and preferably monthly. Then, management should read it.

The cash flow projection is not rocket science. All it displays is cash expected to come in, cash expected to go out, and the difference between the two numbers plus an explanation of how any negative difference will be financed. Exhibits 8.2 and 8.3 are sample cash flow projections.

The key lines are at the bottom, as ever. The Beginning Balance shows the level of indebtedness with which the organization began the month, probably drawing the financing from something like a

Jun	Jul	Aug	Sep	Oct	Nov	Dec
300,000	300,000	300,000	300,000	300,000	300,000	300,000
75,000	75,000	75,000	75,000	75,000	75,000	75,000
13,333	13,333	13,333	13,333	13,333	13,333	13,333
388,333	388,333	388,333	388,333	388,333	388,333	388,333
252,400	252,400	252,400	252,400	252,400	252,400	252,400
25,240	25,240	25,240	25,240	25,240	25,240	25,240
25,240	25,240	25,240	25,240	25,240	25,240	25,240
2,500	2,500	2,500	2,500	2,500	2,500	2,500
1,250	1,250	1,250	1,250	1,250	1,250	1,250
3,000	3,000	3,000	3,000	3,000	3,000	3,000
45,000	45,000	45,000	45,000	45,000	45,000	45,000
1,500	1,500	1,500	1,500	1,500	1,500	1,500
2,000	2,000	2,000	2,000	2,000	2,000	2,000
24,000	26,000	26,000	26,000	26,000	26,000	26,000
3,000	3,000	3,000	3,000	3,000	3,000	3,000
2,000	2,000	2,000	2,000	2,000	2,000	2,000
387,130	389,130	389,130	389,130	389,130	389,130	389,130
1,203	(797)	(797)	(797)	(797)	(797)	(797)
16,015	17,218	16,421	15,624	14,827	14,030	13,233
17,218	16,421	15,624	14,827	14,030	13,233	12,436

Exhibit 8.2 Continued

	Jan	Feb	Mar	Apr	May
CASH IN					
Program Services	300,000	300,000	300,000	300,000	300,000
Fundraising	50,000	50,000	50,000	50,000	50,000
Miscellaneous	13,333	13,333	13,333	13,333	13,333
Total In	363,333	363,333	363,333	363,333	363,333
CASH OUT					
Salaries	227,160	227,160	340,740	227,160	227,160
Payroll Taxes	22,716	22,716	34,074	22,716	22,716
Employee Benefits	22,240	22,240	22,240	22,240	22,240
Consultants	0	0	0	0	2,500
Legal/Audit	0	0	0	1,000	2,000
Contracted Services	3,000	3,000	3,000	3,000	3,000
Program Supplies	47,000	47,000	47,000	47,000	47,000
Vehicle Expense	1,500	1,500	1,500	1,500	1,500
Equipment Leases	1,600	1,600	1,600	1,600	4,000
Rent	24,000	24,000	24,000	24,000	24,000
Utilities	4,500	4,500	4,500	4,500	1,500
Property Insurance	0	0	0	0	0
Total Out	353,716	353,716	478,654	354,716	357,616
Net Inflow (Outflow)	9,617	9,617	(115,321)	8,617	5,717
Beginning Balance	10,000	19,617	29,234	(86,087)	(77,470)
Ending Balance	19,617	29,234	(86,087)	(77,470)	(71,753)

Exhibit 8.3 Reliable Cash Flow Projection

line of credit or transfers from nonoperating funds. The Ending Balance shows the impact of that month's cash loss or gain on the source of financing. By the way, this is a nice cash flow picture for a true line of credit since bankers' own regulations normally stipulate that lines of credit must be down to zero for at least one 30-day period during any one year.

While reading a cash flow projection is not likely to cause someone to break into the intellectual equivalent of a sweat, preparing one might. The accompanying disk includes some files that will be helpful in projecting cash flow. The difference between useful cash flow projections and mediocre ones is largely the amount of planning and thought that goes into their preparation. In turn, the nonprofit manager's job is to be able to recognize and demand good projections.

Three-Zero Projections.   Exhibits 8.2 and 8.3 illustrate the difference between a sloppy and sharp cash flow. Exhibit 8.2 shows the unmistakable signs of "Three-Zero" cash flow projections.

Jun	Jul	Aug	Sep	Oct	Nov	Dec
200,000	150,000	450,000	400,000	300,000	300,000	300,000
75,000	75,000	75,000	75,000	250,000	25,000	75,000
13,333	13,333	13,333	13,333	13,333	13,333	13,333
288,333	238,333	538,333	488,333	563,333	338,333	388,333
340,740	238,809	238,809	358,214	238,809	238,809	358,214
34,074	23,881	23,881	35,821	23,881	23,881	35,821
22,240	22,240	58,240	22,240	22,240	22,240	22,240
0	0	0	5,000	7,500	7,500	7,500
2,000	2,500	2,500	2,500	2,500	0	0
3,000	3,000	3,000	3,000	3,000	3,000	3,000
47,000	47,000	47,000	23,000	47,000	47,000	47,000
1,500	1,500	1,500	1,500	1,500	1,500	1,500
1,600	1,600	1,600	1,600	4,000	1,600	1,600
24,000	26,000	26,000	26,000	26,000	26,000	26,000
1,500	1,500	1,500	1,500	2,500	4,000	4,000
0	0	6,000	6,000	6,000	6,000	0
477,654	368,030	410,030	486,375	384,930	381,530	506,875
(189,321)	(129,697)	128,303	1,958	178,403	(43,197)	(118,542)
(71,753)	(261,074)	(390,771)	(262,468)	(260,510)	(82,107)	(125,304)
(261,074)	(390,771)	(262,468)	(260,510)	(82,107)	(125,304)	(243,846)

Exhibit 8.3 Continued

Everywhere you look in this analysis you see three zeroes—nice, rhythmic calculations that roll soothingly forward like waves in a tropical lagoon. There's only one problem: They're wrong. Financial life doesn't behave that way. Paradoxically, while there are always unforeseen circumstances, a good deal of financial activity is fairly predictable down to the dollar. It is not unreasonable to expect some predictions to be in the hundreds of dollars, even in a nonprofit the size of the one in the exhibit. Good hard thinking about cash behavior tends to have a precision of its own.

Thoughtful Cash Flow Projections. Now look at Exhibit 8.3. Immediately you can see major differences between the two projections. Fund-raising, for example, is much more irregular as a cash source, starting with a lower monthly amount and including a whopping big month in October. We can safely assume that some sort of major fund-raiser is expected for the month of September, with the bulk of cash received in October, or, it's an October cash-based, fund-raising activity.

Salaries seem to fluctuate, but look again. This agency obviously pays its employees every two weeks. For two of every three months, there are only two payrolls. Every third month, however, there are actually three payrolls. This quite predictable variation occurs once each quarter, or every thirteen weeks. Payroll taxes, being calculated on the basis of monthly payrolls, fluctuate in tandem.

Employee benefits are insulated from this type of variation but have their own quirks. A logical inference here is that a pension plan or some form of insurance requires a big one year payment in August, probably in advance of a new policy year beginning September 1. Incidentally, many benefits suppliers offer payment plans that will flatten this kind of peak cash drain, although it will probably cost less to finance it yourself.

With planning, consulting expenses are very predictable. Consultants are also paid in arrears. Looks like big consultations are planned for April and August through November. Audit fees are very predictable, and in the exhibits they seem to be blended with legal costs that are more susceptible to yearly variations.

The organization must expect a fall-off in utilization in August, which will translate into a smaller cash outlay when the bills are paid in September.

Service contracts are often considered part of equipment leasing costs. A big payment is due in May and another in November. Usage adjustment charges might behave the same way, depending on how the lease agreement is written.

Winter in most of the country means higher utility bills, as we can see in the November to April period. Sometimes major utility companies will offer ways to stretch payments over a ten- or even twelve-month period. This helps the cash flow, but at what cost? The operative question is whether you can "borrow" the money cheaper from yourself (especially through careful cash management) or another source at better rates than what the utility company will offer. *Hint:* Usually you can.

Property insurance gets paid in one big bite or a few smaller ones. The financing decision is the same as for utilities.

What It All Means

Time to look at the bottom line again. The story told this time is very different. Instead of a tame cash flow with no accumulated deficit, we have a bit of a beast that registers a projected shortage over $390,000 in July. The difference is that Exhibit 8.3 tells its story in far greater detail than Exhibit 8.2. Which story would you rather hear? Don't answer that question yet. The stakes are high in matters of cash flow. Running out of cash even for a short time can have serious and possibly fatal consequences for a nonprofit. It's always nice to be soothed by the message of Exhibit 8.2 but to do your job properly you need the clarity of Exhibit 8.3. Besides, disasters predicted six or eight months in advance are easier to plan for, and one benefit of doing this kind of projection is that you have plenty of time to alter strategy.

CONCLUSION

Regular cash flow projections ought to be the responsibility of the chief financial person. Use the format in Exhibits 8.2 and 8.3 as a guide, but modify it freely. There is no single correct format.

Many nonprofit financial managers at all sizes of organizations do rudimentary cash flow projections in their heads all the time. The benefit of a formalized, written process is that it puts the information on paper where everybody can see it and act accordingly. What the nonfinancial manager contributes by insisting on a written document is not just getting the job done but communicating the importance of cash management to the organization. Knowing a little about the process adds the ability to distinguish a helpful plan from a mediocre one.

CHAPTER NINE

Capital: Why Capital Is Not a Four-Letter Word

For a major wellspring of financial health—or lack of it—look no further than a nonprofit's capital structure. Its degree of liquidity will determine how fast it can move. Its profitability will determine its ability to sustain itself. But as a barometer of financial vitality, and sometimes as an indication of financial sophistication, the decisions a nonprofit makes about how it acquires and deploys its capital are unsurpassed.

Capital refers to the long-term debt and net assets carried by the nonprofit. The capital structure of a nonprofit is so important that it will help determine how well the organization carries out its day-to-day business. One reason why this happens is that capital buffers an organization from external ups and downs. For instance, owning a capital asset is usually less expensive in the long term than leasing it. More subtly, the greater control that comes with ownership can prevent such institutionally draining crises as having to move every few years because the landlord raises the rent. These are just two ways that a good capital structure insulates an organization from threats to its stability.

There is a popular cynical observation that "money talks," roughly translated as "greed rules." But what that phrase really means is that we talk with money. Every purchase or investment decision is a way of expressing ourselves and our choices. This is why, as noted in Chapter Two, the real bottom line is not revenues minus expenses but rather the ability of the nonprofit to continue to attract money from the outside. As long as a nonprofit can find

119

some way of getting outside capital into the organization, it can usually survive.

A for-profit corporation has three ways of bringing in capital: (1) generating profits, (2) borrowing, or (3) selling a share of ownership. A nonprofit has only the first two, since it cannot sell shares (except in very rare situations). By itself, this prohibition against selling shares—which is an entirely appropriate and necessary part of being granted the special status of tax exemption—radically reduces the chances of the average nonprofit being adequately capitalized. Insuring that it is well capitalized for its mission requires a conscious act of will.

THE MECHANICS OF CAPITAL FINANCING

Before we get too deeply into a nonprofit's potential sources of capital—a far more critical question than is commonly realized—it would be a good idea to cover the mechanics of capital finance. Exhibit 9.1 tells the initial story of a $100,000 loan at 5 percent interest for 20 years, while Exhibit 9.2 displays the same information graphically. The loan has been amortized, or paid off gradually over a period of time. Monthly payments for each of the 240 months of the loan are a steady $659.96, or a yearly total of $7,919.52.

These amounts stay the same throughout the life of the loan, accounting for the straight line at the top of Exhibit 9.2. The composition of the payments, however, changes every month. Exhibit 9.2 tracks these changes over the life of the loan. Each payment is composed of a certain amount of principal (a fraction of the original loaned amount) and a certain amount of interest (the cost of borrowing the money). Because the interest on the loan is recomputed after each month's payment on the basis of a slightly smaller principal, the interest payments start out being much higher than the part of the monthly payment that repays the principal. At the end of the first year, for example, $4,911.83 has been paid in interest while only $3,007.69 has been repaid in principal. Thereafter, the two amounts slowly switch relative positions.

The cash flow created by the loan is an entirely different story at the heart of which is the concept of depreciation. A capital asset can be expected to last for more than a single year. Since the lifetime of

End of Year	Month	Date	Payment	Interest	Principal	Balance
		01-01-19X1				100,000.00
	1	01-30-19X1	659.96	397.26	262.70	99,737.30
	2	02-28-19X1	659.96	415.57	244.39	99,492.91
	3	03-30-19X1	659.96	414.55	245.41	99,247.50
	4	04-30-19X1	659.96	413.53	246.43	99,001.07
	5	05-30-19X1	659.96	412.50	247.46	98,753.61
	6	06-30-19X1	659.96	411.47	248.49	98,505.12
	7	07-30-19X1	659.96	410.44	249.52	98,255.60
	8	08-30-19X1	659.96	409.40	250.56	98,005.04
	9	09-30-19X1	659.96	408.35	251.61	97,753.43
	10	10-30-19X1	659.96	407.31	252.65	97,500.78
	11	11-30-19X1	659.96	406.25	253.71	97,247.07
	12	12-30-19X1	659.96	405.20	254.76	96,992.31
1	totals		7,919.52	4,911.83	3,007.69	96,992.31
2	totals		7,919.52	4,778.26	3,141.26	93,851.05
3	totals		7,919.52	4,617.57	3,301.95	90,549.10
4	totals		7,919.52	4,448.65	3,470.87	87,078.23
5	totals		7,919.52	4,271.06	3,648.46	83,429.77
6	totals		7,919.52	4,084.38	3,835.14	79,594.63
7	totals		7,919.52	3,888.19	4,031.33	75,563.30
8	totals		7,919.52	3,681.94	4,237.58	71,325.72
9	totals		7,919.52	3,465.14	4,454.38	66,871.34
10	totals		7,919.52	3,237.23	4,682.29	62,189.05
11	totals		7,919.52	2,997.67	4,921.85	57,267.20
12	totals		7,919.52	2,745.85	5,173.67	52,093.53
13	totals		7,919.52	2,481.19	5,438.33	46,655.20
14	totals		7,919.52	2,202.95	5,716.57	40,938.63
15	totals		7,919.52	1,910.45	6,009.07	34,929.56
16	totals		7,919.52	1,603.01	6,316.51	28,613.05
17	totals		7,919.52	1,279.85	6,639.67	21,973.38
18	totals		7,919.52	940.16	6,979.36	14,994.02
19	totals		7,919.52	583.10	7,336.42	7,657.60
20	totals		7,865.34	207.74	7,657.60	0.00
	Grand totals		158,336.22	58,336.22	100,000.00	

Exhibit 9.1 Amortization Schedule

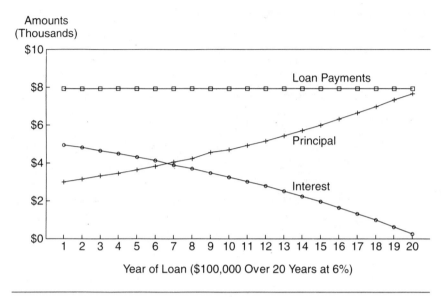

Amounts
(Thousands)

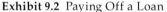

Exhibit 9.2 Paying Off a Loan

a capital asset will cross fiscal years, there needs to be a way to express the idea that each year a "piece" of the asset gets used up or "consumed" in the same way that any other tangible item would be consumed in the course of operations. We need a way to show that the true cost of a capital asset is paid in segments over a number of years. This is the role of depreciation.

The simplest way to express this concept of yearly consumption of part of a capital asset is by dividing the asset's acquisition cost by the number of years it can be expected to last (see Box). Known as the *useful life* of the asset, this time period is established for each type of asset by the Internal Revenue Service. (Sometimes funding sources will insist on a different useful life.) For an asset costing $25,000 with a useful life of five years, the yearly depreciation cost would be $5,000, or $416.67 per month. This amount would be charged automatically each month to the cost of the program using the asset.

Exhibit 9.3 shows the very positive effects on cash flow in the early years of the loan. Cash outflow is stable throughout the life of the loan, since it is simply the same payment each month. Note that we consider only financing costs here, not operations-related costs such as maintenance or repair. The cash inflow side, on the

How Depreciation Is Calculated

Owing to the powerful effect on cash flow and profitability that depreciation charges can have, there are different ways of calculating it. The method referred to in the text is called *straight line depreciation* and is used by virtually all nonprofits. There are other methods and accompanying rationalizations for calculating depreciation in different ways. What they all have in common is that for-profit organizations can use them to accelerate depreciation charges. Higher depreciation charges can mean more cash and less profits, which can in turn change the tax bill. Methods for calculating depreciation are a perennial hot topic with for-profit corporations and their tax advisers, but have little relevance to most nonprofits.

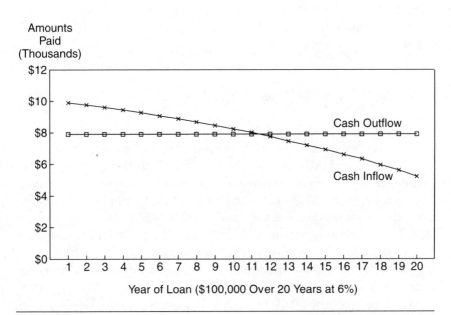

Exhibit 9.3 Cash Flows of a Loan

other hand, actually starts at a point higher than the outflow and then declines throughout the loan's term to reach a level several thousand dollars per year less than the outflow.

The nature of reimbursement for capital costs accounts for the reversal. Assume that all costs associated with the loan itself are fully reimbursed, a good assumption unless the nonprofit has another benevolent source of funding to cover permanent deficiencies. What is actually being reimbursed is not the loan payment itself but rather the depreciation, which we know to be $5,000 per year, plus the actual cost of the interest payments for that year. We also know that depreciation is an expense that does not get paid in cash, so any reimbursement that covers the cost of the service is actually bringing in cash that was not paid out. Therefore, in year one of the loan the actual cash inflow is equal to $5,000 plus $4,912 in interest cost for a total of almost $10,000— this at a time when total cash outflow is only $7,919. By contrast, reimbursement in the final year is the same $5,000 plus a mere $207.74 while the loan payment is the same $7,919.

The pattern sketched here is true for any capital financing, although there are a myriad of modifications and variations possible. Assuming that depreciation and interest payments are somehow fully covered, cash flows will always go from very favorable in the early years to unfavorable at the end of the loan's term.

THE PRESENT VALUE OF MONEY

To the above virtues of capital finance one must also add the effect of the present value of money. This concept is one of those ideas that practically invites complexity even though it is really quite simple. Everyone knows instinctively that $1,000 today is worth more than $1,000 a year from today. Even if we disregard the effects of inflation as well as the possible risk of waiting a year for the money, the fact is that the sooner we can put money to use for us the sooner it will produce benefits. If nothing else, we can put it into a simple interest-bearing account for a year. For example, if we were to put $952.38 into an account paying 5 percent interest compounded yearly it would be worth $1,000 for us in one year.

Another way of looking at it is that $952.38 is today's value of $1,000 in one year at 5 percent interest compounded yearly. Given a choice between a guaranteed $952.38 today or a guaranteed $1,000 in one year, we would be indifferent. If, on the other hand, we felt that we could take that same $952.38 today and put it someplace where it would produce 6 percent interest in one year we would have $1,009.52 instead of $1,000. In finance lingo, the future value of the cash flow is better at the higher interest rate.

This is the kind of thinking that brings structure to capital finance decisions. What is the present value of the projected stream of cash? How much does it change when my assumptions change? What are the alternatives? As might be expected, the same methods of analysis work with purchases as well as with financing. In fact, in any financial setting where regular streams of cash exist, the present value calculation can bring order to what otherwise might seem a jumble of numbers. This same technique can lead to thinking that, taken too far, can betray the mission by focusing exclusively on financial considerations when deciding whether or not to make an investment.

The actual present value formula? No need for it. Go to the nearest computerized spreadsheet package or buy a $30 business calculator and follow the steps laid out in the manual. Or go to the library for a book of tables. Better still, have someone else do it.

SOURCES OF CAPITAL

Nonprofits actually have a relatively large number of sources of capital. It's just that they aren't always labeled that way, nor do they add up to an especially potent capital structure. One of the most common and yet most unacknowledged sources of short-term capital is accounts payable, or the nonprofit's bills that have not yet been paid. This source of capital is covered in Chapter Eight.

Before we go any further, let's acknowledge a central fact: Money is a commodity. Possession of it gets transferred for profit the same way that any other commodity gets transferred for a profit. This means that the more of it that gets transferred and for a longer period of time, the lower the cost to the recipient. Generally, owners of capital want to transfer it in the largest chunks possible and to be guaranteed to receive interest payments on it for the longest period of time possible.

Perhaps not surprisingly, the market for this commodity resembles the market for many others. We might compare the capital distribution system for nonprofits to the way we buy another familiar commodity, milk. At the lowest end of the retail chain is the half pint carton of milk. Somewhere in the middle is the equally familiar gallon container of milk, and at the far end of the spectrum are the institutional multigallon containers used by restaurants and food manufacturers.

That half pint of milk is like the loan for a nonprofit's copier. It's about the smallest amount of money that a lender will want to lend, so the cost per unit of the commodity is high. The retailer is really selling access, as signalled in the milk world by the fact that the typical vendor of that little carton is a convenience store. In the financial world, loans like these may not even be made by traditional banks but rather by specialty leasing or credit corporations.

Commercial banks are the half gallon and gallon milk vendors. Single transactions may not amount to much, but the overall volume of business is significant and profitable. These customers have a bit longer time horizon, or at least a demand for more of the stuff. Gallon containers fit their budgets, storage capacity, and rate of consumption. The milk retailers gear their operations to large numbers of small transactions.

At the high end of this fanciful spectrum are the bulk consumers of milk and capital. No half pints or even grocery carts full of gallons for these consumers. They buy in bulk, demand and get discounts, and are generally comfortable with purchasing and using massive quantities. They may even understand the milk business as well as their milk suppliers but have chosen for whatever reason to concentrate their business energies elsewhere. The nonprofit finance equivalent to these bulk milk purchasers are institutions that can participate in the bulk money market, better known as the bond market. These institutions are the large and sophisticated borrowers of huge amounts of capital. They build massive physical plants and routinely invest heavily in equipment. They tend to be hospitals and universities, mainly because both of these tax-exempt activities require large scale use of both buildings and technology.

THE GREAT DIVIDE AMONG NONPROFITS

Perhaps you can now see the Great Divide among nonprofit organizations, or the line between those with regular access to traditional capital markets and those without. The difference is dimly experienced by the latter as a feeling that their colleagues on the other side of the line are "different" from them, although in exactly what way other than sheer size is usually not clear. A big reason for this feeling of differentness is the fact that, in capital finance terms, they *are* different.

One of the cardinal rules of capital finance is that one must never borrow money for the long-term at short-term rates. Lenders of money for short-term needs know that they will be getting it back in the near future and must then find another borrower under market conditions that no one can predict. Naturally, they will charge more just to cover their higher administrative costs and the risk from uncertainty. Nonprofits without access to the capital market may have to violate that cardinal rule, borrowing money for long-term capital investments at rates geared for short-term returns.

A more likely scenario is that they will have to pay for a middle person to stand between them and the capital markets. This is the role played by the average bank. Because of the economics described earlier, most major capital sources are uninterested and unequipped to loan money to, say, convert a single family house into a small office. Middle persons cost money, so the cost of borrowing that amount of money is higher because it has to be packaged in a smaller amount. The difference may only be a matter of a point or two on the interest rate, but over the long-term that adds up to a lot of money that flows out of the nonprofit for the convenience of borrowing capital.

Borrowing larger amounts of money more directly from the source is preferable, but the problem for most nonprofits is that the economics of this type of capital finance work against them. When capital is sought from banks in small amounts, as it has to be for the majority of nonprofits, the costs of borrowing are higher. The challenge for nonprofits is to constantly try to get as close to the sources of capital as possible. An increasing number of nonprofits are entering the capital markets, but there are still obstacles.

One obstacle is what might be termed historic inertia. Because most nonprofits haven't participated in capital markets, they don't participate now. Except for hospitals and universities, they are frequently not written into enabling legislation for bonding authorities, they're not rated for borrowing by the rating services, and so forth.

A bigger stumbling block is the economics of bonds themselves. A bond is essentially a promise to repay a loan, except that that promise is a written document that can itself be bought and sold. As publicly traded debt instruments, bonds must be highly standardized because bond buyers—often insurance companies and pension funds—cannot afford to spend a lot of time examining all aspects of a bond before purchasing it. This means that bonds have to meet various standards. The cost of meeting those standards such as legal and accounting fees and insurance charges can easily run into six figures. Even though bonds issued by a tax-exempt entity are themselves exempt from tax on the investors' proceeds and therefore the borrower pays less interest, these fixed costs drive up the overall expense of the borrowing. In effect, this means that no bond offering can be less than a few million dollars, putting bond financing out of the reach of the majority of nonprofits. Farsighted nonprofits will also factor in the possible long-term effects of the tax on unrelated business income: Profits realized by the sale of an asset acquired using debt financing trigger the unrelated business income tax, thereby boosting the overall cost of the financing even more.

FUTURE ACCESS TO CAPITAL MARKETS

There are, however, reasons for hope that more nonprofits will gain access to capital markets in the future (see Box). One very good reason is the change in laws governing bond issuance. For years, private industrial and housing developers could use government-backed bonds to finance their projects. But many congressional staffers and legislators objected to what they saw as a funneling of government funds into private hands, and so tax reform legislation in 1984 and 1986 began to severely restrict that form of bond financing. Massachusetts' ceiling, for instance,

Capital Ideas—Innovation in Financing for Nonprofits

Some creative thinking can expand nonprofits' access to lower-cost capital. Here are a few promising ideas:

- *Pooled Bond Issue*
  A handful of similar organizations get together to float a single bond. They share issuance costs and proceeds proportionately, and the bond is sold to the public just like any other investment vehicle.

- *Pooled Pension Funds*
  Another idea much discussed but not yet acted upon in any widespread way is to pool pension funds from a large number of nonprofit employees for the express purpose of purchasing bonds issued by nonprofits.

- *Private Foundations*
  Private foundations in some parts of the country have innovative borrowing programs.

- *Private Bond Offerings*
  Private bond offerings have always been possible, in which a few private investors get together to purchase a bond floated by a particular organization. This approach has the benefit of being somewhat less expensive and free of many of the restrictions imposed on bonds offered for sale to the public although the issuer has to be of substantial enough size to handle the issue.

dropped from $1.5 billion worth of financing in 1985 to $290 million just five years later.

Intentionally or not, the reforms allowed virtually unlimited financing to continue flowing to charitable organizations. Consequently, quasi-public bond authorities and the associated finance professionals who were squeezed out of industrial and housing bonds suddenly found tax-exempt issues much more attractive. Regulations were rewritten to include other forms of nonprofit public charities and the traditional definition of a borrower was liberalized. This shift has begun to eliminate the historic inertia problem.

Simply broadening access does nothing to solve the problem of the underlying economics of bond financing. But even here, there is reason for optimism. Like most other fields, finance has undergone radical transformation in recent years and promises to continue doing so. One director of a bond-issuing agency notes that there are investment banking firms that get 60 percent of their revenue today from financial vehicles that didn't even exist ten years ago.

THE ROLE OF NET ASSETS OR FUND BALANCES

As the nonprofit equivalent of net worth or equity, net assets play a key role in an organization's capital structure. Net assets do not represent money put into the organization but rather the accumulation of yearly surpluses over the history of the corporation. A large net assets amount is not necessarily a goal in itself, but will be the outcome of a prolonged period of profitable management. It should be developed and protected to the maximum extent possible. Grown large enough, it may signal that a nonprofit has the internal resources to reduce its reliance on outside capital.

STRATEGIC CAPITAL MANAGEMENT

Finally, some institutions are responding to their need for additional capital strategically. More and more nonprofits are seriously considering mergers in response to changes in their environment. Access to capital is often one of the driving forces in that decision, although participants usually express it as a need for better facilities, program expansion, and so on, rather than as a financial tactic.

Capital is not a four-letter word. In fact, it underlies much of the way a nonprofit is organized and determines a great deal about its cost effectiveness. Wise managers and board members will pay as much attention to capital structure as they do to profitability. It's the foundation of good financial health, in more ways than one.

CHAPTER TEN

Budgeting: Taming the Budget Beast

W hat inert object strikes fear into the hearts of nonprofit (and for-profit) managers everywhere? It's *the Budget.* It is too bad that it has to be this way. Budgets are supposed to help management, not intimidate it. Budgets are intended as a tool, a means to an end.

Part of the problem is that budgets are often regarded like instant lottery tickets—expend a bit of effort and the number is magically revealed. This approach leaves you wondering where the numbers came from. The real work in budgeting has nothing to do with the numbers that wind up on the final copy of the final version. By the time the budget amounts are published, it's too late to change much anyway. It's what underlies the numbers that counts. Putting the budget together in the first place is where the hard work gets done.

There is a lot written about budgets and budgeting processes, and much of it is simply wishful thinking. Budgets, especially program budgets, get built and approved in a variety of ways that don't always adhere to the theories. Any useful budget had to have been constructed from the ground up at some point. Starting with the numbers in the budget therefore begs the most important question of how the numbers got into the budget in the first place. This chapter will try to deal with exactly that question.

Exhibit 10.1 shows a program budget for the Campaign to Clean Up America's municipal recycling program. This is the kind of presentation you'd expect to see at a management team meeting or as

Revenue	FTE		
Government contracts/grants			375,600
Total In			
Expenses			
	FTE		
Salaries			
Program Director	0.5	37,500	18,750
Promotions specialist	0.3	32,000	10,560
Event coordinator	0.5	30,000	15,000
Drivers	2.5	25,000	62,500
Technicians	2.5	20,000	50,000
Mechanic	0.2	29,000	5,800
Secretarial/Clerical	0.5	24,000	12,000
Relief/Overtime Factor			11,830
Payroll Taxes			15,475
Employee Benefits			11,000
Other			3,000
Consultants			3,000
Advertising			25,000
Supplies			7,000
Vehicle Expense			15,000
Equipment Leases			3,500
Depreciation			3,231
Rent			12,000
Utilities			2,000
Property Insurance			2,500
General & Administrative			86,454
Total Expenses			375,600

Exhibit 10.1   CCUA Municipal Recycling Program Budget

part of a yearly planning document. What we're going to do is to look underneath it to see how the numbers were composed.

PLAYING REVENUES LIKE A SYMPHONY

The top line doesn't get much attention in nonprofit organizations, and for good reason. In the past, most of the action took place in the expense category. That is, since revenues often tend to be predictable (from contracts or grants several months or even years in advance), any change in budget structure necessitates a quick trip to the expense category to find some offsetting adjustments.

CCUA's revenue for the municipal recycling program is, well, boring. This program is contractual in nature, meaning that there is a formal and probably legally binding expectation that CCUA will carry out a series of transactions with each municipality that has a definite beginning and a definite end (with probable extensions of the contract).

Usually the most interesting aspect of revenue portraits is what goes on behind them. In effect, the revenue stream marks what society is willing to put into CCUA, under what terms and conditions, and with what degree of certainty. The real power—or the frustration—of all these different types of revenue streams is the interaction between and among them. The nonprofit manager's role is to learn the differences, appreciate the strengths and weaknesses, and then take maximum advantage of each one according to the situation.

For instance, Medicare is notorious for underpaying many providers. Yet it has two advantages. First, it is *reliable*; as a payer, Medicare usually acts in a straightforward, workmanlike manner. This habit makes it a good payment source. Second, in some settings in some states, it has been relatively underutilized until recently. In those cases, the provider that is just starting to take Medicare patients may actually find it to be the fastest growing payment source, and one thing it is always nice to have is a fast-growing payment source.

Or take CCUA. Those 17 municipal recycling contracts it holds are its single largest chunk of revenue. The CCUA business manager might look at that situation and muse in the following way:

> CCUA's strategic planning process told us that recycling is the major way we want to clean up America, and here we just picked up 17 cost reimbursement recycling contracts fairly easily. Furthermore, it looks like we could add another few dozen without much effort. Generally the municipalities pay steadily but slowly, which means that each new contract is going to require a month or two worth of cash to cover expenses before reimbursements kick in. Since we're not awash in cash, we need to get better cash flow so that we can offset that cashless month or two that each new contract will entail. Now, if I remember correctly, the AllGreen Foundation offers recycling cash flow grants . . . .

Alternatively, the business manager may decide to carry out some of that expansion into recycling via funding sources that offer better cash flow than municipalities' cost reimbursement methods, *even if those other sources have some other undesirable financial aspect.* In this type of situation, there is potential for financial considerations to unduly influence the way the nonprofit carries out its mission. Frankly, however, it requires an unusually strong financial person (or a weak executive) before this risk becomes a real threat. For most situations, keeping this sort of planning scrupulously connected to mission helps keep the nonprofit viable and effective.

EXPENSES

Salaries

The first thing you will notice in Exhibit 10.1 about salary expense is that it is measured in FTEs, or full-time equivalents. This is a handy, though by no means universal way of expressing the cost of one person working full time for 52 weeks. (Yes, there's a way to cover vacation time, but hold that thought.) It's a good way to be sure that personnel expenditures are measured uniformly. To calculate the total cost for the year for a particular position, multiply by the FTEs for that position. Note that the total yearly cost is often the only number that actually appears on the budget; ideally, this is because the multiplication described above is done on unpublished worksheets.

Read a budget's details for the stories they tell. Exhibit 10.1 tells us many things just by the personnel complement. A half-time program director in a program of this size may mean that the same full-time employee is responsible for the municipal recycling program half of the time and another program the other half of the time, responsibility for a program of this size being hard to manage as a part-time employee.

The combination of the promotions specialist and the event coordinator suggests a few themes. For one thing, the municipalities contracting with CCUA obviously believe that part of recycling involves education and that they cannot or will not do it themselves.

It may even be voluntary recycling; if it were mandatory, the towns would have other ways of publicizing the message.

The presence of an event coordinator in a relatively small program budget like this implies a lot about the scope of CCUA's effort. Two and a half drivers and the same number of technicians, along with a mechanic who only works one day a week (0.2 FTE times 40 hours per week) can't cover a lot of ground, environmentally speaking. With the number of municipalities represented here (see Part III of the 990), it is highly unlikely that the program handles weekly recycling chores in more than one or two of them. Therefore, a good part of the reason for the contract's existence must be to hold special events. We can imagine that the promotions specialist and the event coordinator and even the program director probably spend a fair amount of time on one-time-only recycling days, fairs, conferences, and the like. The advertising budget is their tool.

Relief/Overtime

Exhibit 10.1 illustrates another aspect of this program and in the process raises a vexing personnel budgeting question. Sooner or later, one of the drivers is going to go on vacation or get sick or need a few days off for the funeral of a close relative. If this were the type of position that involved, say, long-range planning or reconciling checking accounts, no problem—the work could wait a few days. But in a municipal recycling program, if there is no driver, there is no recycling. And if there is no recycling on a day when it was supposed to occur, there will be a bunch of angry homeowners. Municipalities don't like angry homeowners, so the program must go on even if the driver cannot.

This is the purpose of the relief/overtime line item. On a day when a driver calls in sick, the program director calls the backup driver he was smart enough to recruit for such an eventuality and pays for the backup out of the relief/overtime line. This line also covers other necessary overtime payments. Before getting into exactly how it does that, however, it is necessary to make a brief digression into the world of labor laws. Almost 60 years ago, Congress passed and the president signed the Fair Labor Standards Act (FLSA). One of the things the FLSA and its later amendments did was to stipulate that workers who put in more than 40 hours per week of work must get paid overtime, or 1.5 times a basic hour's pay, for the 41st hour onward. This provision was intended as a penalty to the employer and an incentive to avoid the sweatshop environment of the early industrial period in our country. At the same time, the FLSA recognized that for some occupations it was impractical or undesirable to adhere to such a standard. Professionals, administrators, and certain types of salespeople are good examples of this group; they are known as exempt employees.

Everyone without a good reason for being exempt from the requirements of the FLSA ("good" being defined by FLSA itself) is considered a nonexempt employee, and the provisions of the FLSA apply fully. Nonprofit corporations are *not* exempt merely because of their tax status. Exemptions are decided only on the basis of individual employees or classes of employees. In the CCUA's municipal recycling program, the drivers, technicians, and mechanic are nonexempt employees, and therefore any work time greater than 40 hours must be compensated at 1.5 times their normal hourly rate. The secretary/clerk may very well be considered nonexempt too, but it is probably a safe bet that the secretary/clerk will not actually incur overtime since it should be possible to share any extraordinary workload with other CCUA secretaries or clerks.

With this as background, it is possible to dig deeper into the recycling budget to see how its creators envision using relief or overtime funds. A quick calculation ($11,830/($62,500 + $50,000 + $5,800)) suggests that they used a flat 10 percent as the factor for relief and overtime. To budget veterans, 10 percent of anything has the smell of a conventional guess, so let's see what it really buys.

Assuming that the relief factor was calculated with the expectation that it would apply equally to all three positions, and in view of the fact that the average salary for the three positions (see the Per FTE column) is $11.86 per hour ($25,000 + $20,000 + $29,000/52 weeks/120 hours per week), the line as funded will purchase 997 hours of substitute labor at straight time.

Most employers give employees vacation time, sick time, and holidays as paid time off. In the case of holidays, recycling crews aren't going to work since the municipality itself is usually considered closed except for essential services. That means that we don't need to cover holidays via the relief/overtime budget. If sick time is earned at a rate of, say, one day per month—and if there is some sort of reasonable cap on the amount of sick time employees can accumulate, as there really should be—then the heaviest call on the relief budget will be for no more than 12 days out of a possible 250 days per year, or about 5 percent.

Our 10 percent relief budget looks healthy at this point. Although that provision for accumulating sick time could be a concern depending on where the cap is set, one could still expect no more than a single employee to hit the cap in any one year, which gives CCUA some good protection. Plus, people working in these types of positions tend not to stay long enough to develop budget-busting levels of sick time anyhow. Also working in CCUA's favor is that individuals working as part of a two-person team typically are less motivated to call in sick frivolously and put extra burden on a partner they will have to face upon returning to work.

Finally, if we assume that the mechanic, only a 0.2 FTE employee, is replaceable in some other way (another mechanic from the agency, for instance, or a cooperative local repair shop), then the relief pool grows higher.

On the other hand, overtime will drive things in a completely different direction. Remember that overtime pay must be 150 percent of the normal hourly rate. Under these terms, the maximum time available from the relief/overtime line would have to be calculated at 1.5 times the average $11.86 salary described earlier, or $17.79 per hour. At this higher hourly rate, the maximum hours available from the budget as overtime with no spending whatsoever on straight time relief is a mere 664 hours.

A minor digression from a digression. For many employers, especially nonprofit organizations, it is popular to give overtime as time off. Doing so properly, unfortunately, is difficult. First of all, the time off has to be calculated according to the same 1.5 multiple, so an hour of overtime must be compensated with an hour and a half of time off. Second, payment must be made or time off taken in the same pay period. These strictures make time off in lieu of pay problematic, to say the least.

This line can get hit from two different directions. We have no way of knowing what mix of relief and overtime pay CCUA is expecting to use with this small amount, but given what we know about the program, it is fair to surmise that they will tend toward straight time replacement costs and try to keep overtime under strict control. This is a typical strategy for most nonprofits and, for that matter, for most small businesses.

What we have just done is to build the relief/overtime line item from scratch. In practice, most organizations will quickly develop rules of thumb for budget planning, such as the 10 percent factor used here. Some rough planning indices may even be available from trade associations and the like in industries where relief or overtime are major budget issues. The idea is to use whatever legitimate shortcuts are available, but continually subject them to tests of usefulness and accuracy.

Payroll Taxes

No good deed goes untaxed, and the act of giving people jobs is no exception. Even tax-exempt organizations must pay when it comes to payroll taxes, though there is a break or two to be had. The first and foremost payroll tax is the Federal Income Continuance Act (FICA), better known as Social Security. This one has grown more complicated in recent years, but in essence the employer pays a flat percentage (currently 7.65 percent) of the first $60,000 or so in wages, and the employee kicks in the same. Years ago large numbers of nonprofits were allowed to opt out of the system, but that changed in 1984 and now virtually all organizations must participate.

Then there's unemployment insurance. While the federal government demands an unemployment tax from proprietary corporations, public charities are exempt. States have their own unemployment tax systems, however and, although it will differ from state to state, the thrust of it will be a percentage tax on payroll. Occasionally states will allow nonprofit public charities to get out of the unemployment insurance system, but in return the agency must agree to pay claims as they come due. It's called self-insurance and is a good way to save money as long as one's payments are less than what would have been paid using the conventional method.

Another tax on payroll takes the form of yet another social insurance program. Like unemployment, the Worker's Compensation system is administered by each state. It's hard to generalize about individual states' methods but for these purposes we don't have to. Worker's Compensation insurance will show up as a bite out of payroll paid for by the employer.

There may be other taxes, especially city taxes, in various localities. Good budgets take these into account. Again, program budgeters usually don't have to blaze financial management trails, so the best method of budgeting for payroll taxes is to use the same organization-wide percentage that other programs have historically spent.

Independent Contractors versus Employees

One popular way of escaping payroll taxes is to pay individuals as independent contractors rather than salaried or wage-earning employees. The advantage of this strategy is that the employer doesn't have to pay payroll taxes or report anything very complicated to the Internal Revenue Service since the employee does it all. The disadvantage is that improperly characterizing employees as independent contractors can get an organization into—this is a technical term—a whole bunch of trouble.

In matters of employment, just saying it doesn't necessarily mean it's true. Just because someone is called an independent contractor or consultant doesn't mean that that is what they are. Ultimately, the decision as to whether a given employment relationship is one or the other depends on the facts and circumstances involved. This means that it is not possible to make sweeping pronouncements that will be valid in every case.

There are, however, some guidelines employers can use. Generally speaking, independent contractors or consultants arrange with an employer to do certain work according to their own methods and without being subject to the control of others. The employer's *right* to control the details and means of an individual's work is a key determinant here; whether the employer actually exercises that right or not is irrelevant. In a true contractor relationship, the employer controls only *what* gets done. *How* it gets done is up to the contractor.

As you might imagine, issues of control are at the heart of the independent contractor vs. employee issue. To supply general guidance in determining which type of relationship exists in any given situation, the IRS offers 20 factors as indicators, outlined in Exhibit 10.2. It should be noted that these factors are useful not as absolute screens but more as insights into the way the government will think about specific cases. The overall picture presented is more important than any one indicator.

Note that the first four factors, taken together, sketch the major features of most employment relationships. Regulatory types frequently refer to the portrait drawn by these factors as the duck test—if it looks like a duck, walks like a duck, and quacks like a duck, then in all probability it is a duck. Still, we have sixteen other factors.

The checklist in Exhibit 10.2 is a reasonably good guide to the government's thinking about who is an employee and who is an independent contractor. Why is this an important question? Both the Internal Revenue Service and the Department of Labor, as enforcers of FLSA, have the right to impose stiff penalties on employers who are not in compliance. Being sure that your nonprofit meets all of the guidelines is not only good budgeting, it's good business too.

Benefits

Of all the areas in the typical budget, employee benefits have changed the most in recent years. Typically the largest single benefit cost is health insurance, and in small nonprofits as well as in comparable small businesses, health insurance can be so expensive that it eats up almost all of the benefits budget allocation.

Various insurance coverages tend to rank next in frequency of offering. Life insurance is a big one, not necessarily because it's desired by large numbers of employees but because it tends to be among the least expensive benefits and because in some cases insurance companies bundle life insurance with other types of coverage to make an overall program more economically feasible for them. Short- and long-term disability insurance coverage is also popular, as is dental insurance. Pension plans are also very popular, and growing more so with the aging of the nonprofit baby boomer generation.

Incidentally, one method for coping with the high cost of benefits starts with the IRS. Section 125 plans, so named for their location in the code, allow employers a range of money-saving alternatives. At the low end of the spectrum is what is variously

_____ 1. *Location.* Under normal circumstances, requiring the person to perform services on your premises is a strong signal that the employer controls the relationship.

_____ 2. *Continuing relationship.* Some sort of ongoing relationship with the person providing the services shows the IRS that an employer-employee relationship functionally exists. Note that it's possible to have a continuing *irregular* relationship where services are delivered frequently.

_____ 3. *Full time required.* True contractors are free to work for whom they want and when they want. If the nonprofit requires the person delivering the services to work all or substantially all of his or her time for that nonprofit and thereby effectively prevents the person from doing any other work for other groups, it's taken as a strong sign that an employer-employee relationship exists.

_____ 4. *Regular hours.* There can be few more convincing signs of control than to require the individual to work at specific times.

_____ 5. *Integration.* When the contractor's services are essential parts of the nonprofit's offerings, the contractor is held to be integrated into operations in a manner characteristic of employees. For instance, one home health agency lost an argument with the IRS over whether its nurses and other therapists were private contractors because it received Medicare payments and therefore the nurses and therapists were required to be in place by Medicare regulations.

_____ 6. *Personal services.* Contractor relationships are typically based on results, employment relationships on methods and results. If a contractor must deliver the services personally, this is seen as evidence that the nonprofit concerns itself with the methods and not just the results.

_____ 7. *Set patterns of work.* Again on the theme of methods, if the nonprofit stipulates that the work is to be done in a specific order or a formalized pattern, the person is regarded as under a degree of control incompatible with independent contractor status.

_____ 8. *Reports, oral or written.* Requiring that the individual submit regular written or oral reports to the organization suggests a certain amount of control.

_____ 9. *Right to terminate.* Contractors are usually bound by contract to deliver a product or an array of services. Employees, on the other hand, can terminate the relationship at any time.

_____ 10. *Right to discharge.* Employees are controlled by the threat of dismissal. Contractors' employers cannot discharge a contractor who is performing according to the previously agreed upon standards without being in breach of contract.

Exhibit 10.2. Checklist: Independent Contractor versus Employee

_____ 11. *Work done for others.* Someone who performs significant work for other firms at the same time is held to be a consultant or contractor.

_____ 12. *Possibility of profit or loss.* Real contractors can gain profit or suffer loss as a result of their work.

_____ 13. *Source of equipment and materials.* One of the hallmarks of independent contractors is that they furnish all of their own tools and materials. Employees get their tools and materials from the employer.

_____ 14. *Provision of training.* If an organization requires a contractor to participate in training sessions or do such things as work closely with an experienced employee, this is taken as a sign that it insists the work be done a certain way.

_____ 15. *Instructions.* Following along the same theme, if the nonprofit can spell out details about how and when a contractor is supposed to work, the relationship is taken as an employer/employee relationship. Note that, as above, the key concept here is that the employer has the right to instruct, not that the employer actually does it.

_____ 16. *Relationship to assistants.* Who hires, supervises, pays and fires assistants? If the individual does it, a contractor relationship is presumed to exist; if it's the nonprofit, then its an employee arrangement.

_____ 17. *Payment method.* Employees get paid on a regular basis such as hourly, weekly or monthly. Contractors, on the other hand, are paid by the job.

_____ 18. *Expense reimbursement.* Normally, employees will be reimbursed for business expenses such as travel. The existence of expense reimbursement is regarded as a tip-off to an employment relationship since employers usually have the right to regulate an employee's business activities.

_____ 19. *Business investment.* Contractors generally must invest in facilities that employees have provided to them. An office rented at fair market value is a good example of this category. Therefore, the absence of a significant business investment of this nature is often a sign of an employee.

_____ 20. *Services available to general public.* Contractors can and must offer their services to the public at large, whereas employees generally are limited to one or perhaps two specific organizations.

Exhibit 10.2. Continued

called a premium conversion or salary reduction plan, in which the dollars previously removed from an employee's paycheck to pay part of the health insurance premium get removed *before* taxes instead. This action has the effect of increasing employee's take home pay since they no longer pay FICA on the money that goes to their premium. It saves FICA payments for the employer too, which makes it a win-win situation for everyone but the federal government.

Next along the spectrum are flexible spending accounts (FSAs), in which the employee sets aside an individually tailored portion of the monthly paycheck, also pretax, to be "deposited" in a "spending account" for use with health expenses or dependent care needs. At the high end is the more familiar idea of cafeteria plans, in which employees get all of the preceding advantages plus the choice of taking some or all of them in the cash equivalent.

Some friendly advice—the area of benefits planning is extraordinarily complex. These descriptions don't even begin to touch on the subtleties of these arrangements, and the details tend to change regularly anyway. It's best to consult a professional before making serious moves in this part of the budget. Fortunately, it's also worth it.

The budget category of fringe benefits is as notable for what it does *not* include as what it does include. Most people assume that this is the budget category that encompasses tuition assistance, time off, and the office picnic. For different reasons in each case, it does not. The federal government applies certain guidelines to fringe benefits that are actually fairly restrictive. Tuition assistance, for instance, is not considered a fringe benefit but an operational expense. Time off gets handled as described in the personnel budgeting section, and the office picnic has to be covered via a line item that might read "Seasonal Personnel Development" or perhaps "Office Communications Expense," total candor sometimes being a handicap in these matters.

As with payroll taxes, budgeting for fringe benefits can be most easily accomplished in an organization with a track record simply by referring to the past. For planning purposes, a standard percentage of salaries and wages should be sufficient, although it should be noted that recently the cost of fringe benefits has gone up more both relatively and in absolute terms than the cost of payroll taxes.

Other Direct Expenses

All other direct expenses (lines "Other" through "Property Insurance") will be different each year for each program. Perhaps the most significant commentary about the rest of the direct expenses is not *what* they are but *that* they are. At a minimum, it's the responsibility of budgeters to capture all of the costs associated with a program, and the place to deposit them is after personnel costs and before general and administrative costs.

Notice that these direct costs show up here, meaning that they can easily and directly be attributed to program services. They are, in a sense, the donut; indirect costs—or general and administrative costs—are the hole. And the shape and size of that hole is the single biggest debating point in nonprofit financial management.

INDIRECT (GENERAL AND ADMINISTRATIVE) COSTS

In any operation, there are costs that are not the direct and exclusive responsibility of any one program or service division. The executive director's salary, for instance, pays for a level of effort that cannot be attributed to a specific program because it was expended on behalf of the nonprofit as a whole. Payroll processing costs from an outside payroll service are another good example of an expense not attributable to direct service.

Theoretically, a huge accounting system and large amounts of staff time and patience could make indirect costs disappear. Everything would be charged directly to program services. Every ten minutes the executive director spent in a meeting, every pencil the bookkeeper picked up to scribble an accounting note, every kilowatt that flowed into the organization's headquarters would be tracked and properly allocated to a specific service.

But does this really matter? Not only do we not need that level of detail to manage operations, the compromises and estimates that the whole scheme would entail would make any output misleading and possibly dangerously unreliable.

Now go in the other direction. Striving for the maximum degree of simplicity and convenience, one might forget about dividing up (allocating) most expenses and instead throw them into a big pool called *indirect costs*. Then, to get each different service to carry its own weight, figure out what portion of that pool should be assigned to each individual service or program. This would be a whole lot simpler than painstakingly coding each bill according to which service should pay it.

These are extremes. But they indicate the two poles between which nonprofit budgeting for indirect costs must play. Being reasonable types, we might be inclined to split the difference and attempt to find the elusive happy medium. Mathematically and accounting-wise this strategy may be perfectly acceptable, but it fails because it ignores human nature.

No one likes administrative costs, especially people who give money to nonprofit organizations that are expected to do good things with that money. To the average donor, money for administration buys paperwork and photocopies of paperwork, not active problem solving and services in support of the mission. Oversimplifying only slightly, a low indirect cost rate signals responsible administration to the average observer, while a high rate suggests waste.

Still, what are administrative costs? In the absence of funding sources' mandatory definitions, administrative costs are largely what you make them. This means that they are determined by a combination of accounting judgments and the capacity of administrative systems.

One final note on administrative cost behavior. A certain level of administrative cost is inevitable. One needs a central office and a financial operation of some size, and there are many other expenses that cannot easily be charged directly to programs but that are necessary regardless of how much direct service is provided. As a result, small nonprofits usually have the highest percentage of administrative expenses. Conversely, as a nonprofit grows, it often can add many more programs with only a modest increase in administrative cost. The secret is knowing that this dynamic exists, and how to manage it.

In our experience, most nonprofit executives are sincerely cost conscious when it comes to administrative expenses. They try to control administrative expense, and if they can't it's probably because they can't control other expenses either. In the end, the governing force in reporting nonprofit administrative expenses is the environment in which the organization operates. If the environment signals through formal or informal means that it wants administrative expense reporting handled in a certain way, over time that is exactly what will happen.

Some funding sources do more than signal. Government, especially the federal government, will define exactly what costs are considered acceptable and to what degree. The federal government goes so far as to give large or recurring providers of service individualized overhead rates to be used in all contracts and grants. Frequently, government programs will put a cap on the amount of overhead they are willing to pay. Nonfederally funded programs may have a similar experience with other government funders, and most nonprofits ultimately need to be aware of how the average person will interpret their administrative cost policies anyway, since the average person may be their next donor.

CONCLUSION

In most settings, budgets and budgeting are overly feared exercises. With the proper knowledge they can be used as the management aids they are intended to be. Budgets can surely be beasts, but only when their human handlers demand it.

CHAPTER ELEVEN

Pricing: How Much *Should* It Cost?

In the end, price is nothing more than a barrier to service, and the art of pricing is deciding how high or low to set that barrier. Other factors can be barriers too, such as geography, cultural considerations, and political realities. But few will doubt that pricing is usually the last and most carefully attended hurdle to clear for those desiring a particular service.

What drives consumers to seek a specific service is the value they expect from it. Museums offer the chance to explore a different culture, social clubs the opportunity to relax with others who have similar interests and tastes, and schools the potential of broadened intellectual experience and possibly higher earning power. Each of these types of programs carries an explicit price that a potential consumer must evaluate before deciding to utilize it. These evaluations range from relatively long and considered deliberations about school enrollment to seconds when it comes to emergency services.

In each case, the underlying dynamic is the same: Pricing decisions are merely the arena for a systematic public dialogue about the value of a service. The nonprofit manager's challenge is to step out from being a bystander in this process and to influence it constructively and proactively.

To do so, it is necessary to understand how nonprofit pricing works. One way to understand the pricing process is along the following continuum:

←——————————————————————————————————————→
Commodity   Specialty

Services whose essential nature place them toward the commodity end of this continuum have a dime-a-dozen quality about them. They are plentiful, more or less standardized in the eye of the consumer, and easily accessed. Day care centers and community residences are examples of commodity services. The combination of regulatory demands, economics, and the nature of the service itself make one version tend to resemble most others.

This is painful for nonprofit managers to consider. It is extremely difficult for someone deeply involved in the actual delivery of a service to regard it as anything other than a uniquely and intensely crafted experience. The fact that there may be thousands of other such experiences appears to negate the individuality of the effort. In reality, however, the consumer may not be able to tell the difference between versions of the service or may regard any differences as unimportant. Either way, choices tend to be made on the basis of something other than perceived value. That other basis is usually price.

This is why services near the commodity end of the continuum cannot raise their price easily. Having no perceived uniqueness in the consumer's mind, they can and will be replaced over time by consumers making choices based solely on price. Here, the consumer is very strong, and the average price will tend to rise only as far as the consumer(s) is willing to let it.

Not so at the high end. A whole different set of factors allows these nonprofits to set their own prices, or more accurately, to govern the spending that will result in higher prices. Add formidable barriers to entry such as major capital investments, and you have a prescription for high prices. On this side of the continuum, the consumer is a lot less powerful. The higher perceived value means he or she *must* have it, while the barriers to entry dampen the supply. The result is much more control for the providers of the service.

Two other factors have historically combined to keep nonprofit prices down. First, decision makers in nonprofit organizations tend to be professionals, and professionals need people identified as service recipients in order to perform professionally. Reimbursement considerations aside, physicians must have patients, teachers must have students, and curators need museum-goers. As professionals, their interests are served by lowering prices as much as possible. This is why the most bitter opposition to a nonprofit corporation's price hike often comes from inside the organization itself.

The second downward force on nonprofit pricing has been the typical means of setting the prices. Since most people used to believe—erroneously—that being a nonprofit organization meant making no profit, price in the nonprofit sector came to be equated with cost. Determine the cost of the service, and you've determined the price. The added economic benefit of tax exemption only made the overall economic bargain irresistible. This type of thinking led naturally to what is called *retrospective pricing*, or pricing that is based on historic spending. Retrospective pricing was common in the health care system; let us know what it cost you to provide the service, said the payers, and we'll pay you a future rate derived directly from that historic record. For providers in a retrospective system, the central beauty is that it is essentially risk-free, a state of affairs more or less happily accepted in return for the inherent aggravations of the daily operations of such a system. Besides, most of the really tedious and aggravating work gets done by outside advisors anyway, and the smart provider will hire a former government pricing specialist to deal with his old colleagues.

Today, the trend in any field where government or some form of management specialists are primary payers is toward prospective pricing. Prospective pricing systems are best developed in the health and social service field, but all share the same unifying theme; they set the price of a given service *before* it's delivered, and do not look to recoup excess payments or supplement losses after the fact. The move toward prospective pricing is the result of a complex set of economic, social, and political variables interacting to produce certain pricing structures as a logical result. Mostly, prospective pricing is disguised under pseudonyms. It's better known as health maintenance organizations, diagnosis related groups, capitation payments, or class (group) rates.

In all of these methodologies, prices are predetermined. To be effective in the long-term, the prices must have at least some relationship to cost, at least the aggregate cost incurred by the industry to produce the required services. But they need not have any direct relationship to the cost structure of any one provider of service. The power of prospectively determined prices is that they tend to drive everyone toward the same average, unless an individual organization can find the means to supplement the basic service.

The effect of this change is to shift risk from the consumer to the provider. Most obvious of the risks is the chance that someone will have guessed wrong about the proper level of pricing. This possibility puts pressure on the provider to monitor costs and pay careful attention to service management, which is exactly what the payers wanted in the first place.

More subtly, the shift to prospective pricing puts far greater pressure on the service provider's management systems. Surviving in a prospective system requires tighter and more efficient management control systems that operate with full knowledge of industry trends. Even more subtle, retrospective payers and their providers must engage each other individually. Typically, they develop a bond. It may be an ambiguous bond, and it may even be rooted in mutual dislike or misunderstanding, but it's a bond nevertheless. Payers in a prospective system tend to have less individual interaction, regarding providers more like commodities while making policy changes that affect whole categories of organizations. Consequently, the class payer can be less of an advocate in certain circumstances.

PRICING METHODOLOGIES

As summarized in Exhibit 11.1, there are many different names and descriptive phrases applicable to payment arrangements, and they vary by locality and area of service. More important, they carry different types of risks and rewards. These types of revenue agreements are discussed next with no particular importance attached to the order.

Fee for Service

The most basic of reimbursement types, fee for service is an exchange of service for money. The price is agreed to beforehand,

Type of Payment	Typical Example	Nature of Risk	Possibility of Profit	Comments
Fee for Service	College tuition, Medicaid (varies by state)	Overestimate market, lose control of costs	Excellent	The classic way toward financial wellbeing
Cost-Based Reimbursement	State or local government contracts	Lose money when actual spending varies from signed budget	None	Requires excellent planning, superb monitoring; good for new or unpredictable services
Unit Reimbursement	Same	Post-contract audits; political fall-out from changed plans	Good	Needs good purchasing systems in place to support purchaser and provider
Class Rates	Same	Costs higher than most peers would cause losses	Good	Best for average cost, average quality nonprofits or those with relatively lower costs
Fixed Price or Project-Based	Federal contracts	Underestimate true project costs	Good	Good for start-ups willing to risk a loss or market leaders good at gauging and carrying out projects
Voucher	Experimental	Marketing failure	Good	Still an experimental approach, but has the potential to become popular in the future; watch carefully
Standard Pricing	Open market	Same	Excellent	Most appealing to entrepreneurial managers; requires staying power

Exhibit 11.1 Pricing Strategies

although exactly who determines the price will vary. When government is a substantial purchaser, it tends to insist on setting the price. When government is a minority or nonexistent purchaser, market pricing will typically dominate. There is no real or implied promise to go beyond a single transaction, nor is there any guarantee of a certain level of service utilization. Fee for service revenue comes with the fewest strings attached about how it can be spent, and it offers an excellent possibility of profit. Most consumer services, from manicures to shoe shines, are fee for service. In the nonprofit sector, it tends to be most heavily used in health care.

Cost-Based Reimbursement

The governing principle of cost reimbursement might be called "Give a Receipt and Get Some Green." Costs are reimbursed only when it can be proved that the money was spent, and then only within the restrictions of a previously approved budget. One of the obvious advantages of this method is that it is quite simple in concept and narrowly focused. It is also completely divorced from utilization, which makes it an ideal reimbursement method in start-up situations or when it is not possible to quantify the services (consultation and education, for example) in any meaningful way.

Cost-based reimbursement can be rigid and unforgiving, especially when you've lost the receipt. Also, it leaves the purchaser inherently in arrears to the provider, who has to come up with a way to support the cash flow until the bill has been rendered, considered, and paid. Cost reimbursement leaves no room for profit and, depending on how it is administered, it can leave lots of room for loss. It must occur in the context of a contract or other official relationship since it involves careful and sustained bookkeeping.

Unit Reimbursement

An alternative to the sharp edges of cost reimbursement is a unit-based reimbursement system. Yearly costs are broken into small pieces based on the natural form of measurement for the service (an hour of counseling, a single day in a residential program, one laboratory test). The nonprofit then delivers one unit of that service and gets paid the predetermined value of the unit. Note that the emphasis is on results—services delivered—not on the actual cost to deliver that unit of service.

Unit reimbursement is very similar to fee for service reimbursement, except that a unit of service reimbursement agreement is usually part of a long-term contract. As a result, the nonprofit has some level of guarantee that it will have many such transactions; therefore, the unit method of reimbursement becomes significant mainly as a planning tool.

Class Rates

The way the price of the unit of service is determined can also have something to say about how the revenue stream gets treated. When some third party—often a government agency or third-party payer—decides it will pay the same price for a unit of service regardless of who delivers it, where, or when, they are structuring what is often known as a class rate.

Class rates are best used when the service being delivered is commodity-like and relatively small, such as an hour of counseling or a day in a program. They free the payer from the minutiae of setting individualized rates and allow the payer to exercise control over operations by managing cost and utilization information. Association membership dues are frequently class rates, as in "members with 1 to 50 employees pay $X per year, those with 51 to 100 pay $Y."

Often class rates are set at the median or the mean of the class, which pressures high-priced nonprofits to cut costs and come closer to the average cost of all participants. And that is precisely the point.

Fixed Price or Project-Based

Although they are more common in the for-profit world of professional services, fixed price revenue arrangements are also possible. Typically, this type of payment accompanies a distinct project with definable outputs—say, a report written or a playground constructed. This methodology puts the risk of budget overruns completely on the nonprofit and thereby benefits the payer. It can also favor the well-run and tightly controlled nonprofit.

Vouchers

A potentially powerful development in government-funded programs is the use of vouchers as a purchasing strategy. Typically, vouchering systems either pay a service provider directly on behalf of an eligible client, reimburse consumers for expenses they incur in utilizing a provider, or take the form of cash assistance. Considering that dwindling government resources and consumer empowerment represent independently compelling agendas, vouchers may be the surprise payment mechanism of the future. States such as New York, Pennsylvania, Minnesota, Maine, Kansas, and Idaho have all experimented with some sort of vouchering system.

Voucher systems of purchasing and pricing could have a dramatic effect on service providers. While the administrative technology for vouchering is currently underdeveloped, the voucher dynamic gives consumers a major voice in service design and delivery and could even result in the elimination of agency-provided services as consumers choose family members as service providers instead. It is a dynamic worth watching.

Standard or Market Pricing

Most pleasing of all, from a revenue point of view, are the opportunities when the nonprofit can price with regard to the market without considering the binding opinions of third parties. These days it's a rare luxury, although when YMCA's set health club membership prices they can sometimes price according to what the local market will bear rather than what the service actually costs.

Market pricing is good when it's possible—and when it doesn't impede the tax-exempt mission. Often when there exists a genuine market for a service partly filled by for-profits, a nonprofit will have lower costs and can therefore price at or below prevailing rates. This leads to rumblings about unfair competition, a charge made from time to time by for-profit companies. For a number of reasons, however, nonprofits and for-profits do not typically compete head-to-head, so the unfair competition concern will probably be confined to only one or two segments of the market.

GOING THE OTHER WAY—CONTRACTUAL
ADJUSTMENTS AND SUBSIDIES

It is important to note that all of the above forms of revenue methods except for fee for service presume the existence of a large institution on the paying end. Increasingly in every field where nonprofits are active, those payers are beginning to throw their economic weight around by demanding discounts and preferential treatment.

A common form of discount is what is euphemistically called a *contractual adjustment,* which is to say an agreement to slice a certain percentage off each bill. In effect, contractual adjustments are merely disguised cost shifting; a consumer responsible for 60 percent of your revenue who demands a contractual adjustment to 50 percent is paying $5/6$ of its share, or 83 percent, while the remaining 40 percent of the purchasers must carry the other half of the load, or 125 percent of their fair share. Is this fair? The question could be debated endlessly, but it doesn't matter—it's real.

Finally, nonprofit organizations often choose to subsidize consumers. This subsidy will take the form of sliding fee scales, discounts for children or the elderly or handicapped or other groups, or outright grants. Subsidy pricing is nothing more than cost shifting in which one party adds a bit to full price in order to offset the lower price that another party receives. If the market will not support such premium pricing, then outside revenue sources must make up the difference. Managers need to recognize that subsidy pricing requires them to play a mediator role in a small-scale resource redistribution effort.

PRICING STRATEGIES

We have put all of these considerations together in Exhibit 11.2 which shows the varying pricing strategies typically used by major types of nonprofits. The vertical axis shows the value of each type of organization's services as typically perceived by *the public in general,* as opposed to consumers or providers of the service. The horizontal axis shows the degree to which providers of the service need to invest in a substantial amount of assets in order to provide the service.

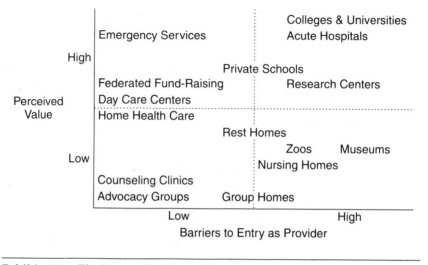

Exhibit 11.2   The Nonprofit Pricing Map

These two axes were chosen because perceived value is an essential—perhaps *the* essential—ingredient in determining how
much people are willing to pay for any service. Equally important
in determining nonprofit pricing is the amount of tangible assets
one must have to enter or stay in the business.

This is important for three reasons. First, the higher costs associated with obtaining and using the assets—buildings in the case
of all high-capital entries on the map, as well as sophisticated technology in many of them—boosts prices. More pertinent, however,
is the fact that the need for capital assets serves as a very effective
barrier to possible new entrants. Not only will established
providers in a capital-intensive field tend to have lower operational
costs associated with their asset base, but the very structure of the
tax-exempt corporation works against new entrants. Remember,
nonprofit corporations cannot have shareholders. Therefore, there
is no possibility of selling shares to new shareholders to raise capital for investing in assets. New entries, then, must find other
sources of funding willing to make grants for capital acquisition,
and these are precisely the most difficult funding sources to find.
Add to that the fact that most proven funding sources are unlikely
to support the entry of new groups in favor of the established panel
of recipients, and the odds against new entrants' success are very
high.

Hospitals solved this type of problem in the 1950s with federal Hill-Burton funding, and colleges and universities have had substantial federal scientific grant programs that served the same purpose. Both types of funding allowed significant investment in capital assets at a critical period for many of today's most powerful and prestigious institutions. At the moment, they are also gone or dwindling.

A third aspect of the logic of nonprofit pricing is rooted in competition or, more accurately, the lack of it. Without federal funding and with substantial growth in for-profit providers in some of the high capital areas, the panel of nonprofit providers in the capital-intensive end is effectively closed. How many universities do you recall getting started in the 1980s? As a result, existing players are that much more likely to be able to get the prices they charge.

A final characteristic of the nonprofit pricing topography in general is that groups with low capital needs tend to exist for the use of a relatively small segment of the population at a time of acute need, while those on the high end of the capital need spectrum touch large numbers of people. Further, those on the low capital end often deal more with lower income populations, while middle-class clientele either use one of the right-side providers today or expect that they will have to do so eventually.

HOW TO PRICE

So how does a nonprofit provider of any kind of service go about pricing? For a specific organization, the objective is to move northward on the map. That is, specific organizations should strive to create a public perception of high value, allowing them to charge a higher price, at least to their nongovernmental payers. A day care center affiliated with a prestigious university may be able to charge more than a nonaffiliated peer. A museum with an especially timely exhibit might be able to charge separately for that admission. One museum boosted its revenue with a *Dinosaurs of Jurassic Park* exhibition featuring actual props from the film shortly after it was released.

At the same time, single nonprofit organizations generally should refrain from moving eastward on the map without uniquely strong protection in the form of patents, geography, or some other such buffers, simply because it is very hard (not to mention ethically questionable) for a single organization to so dominate its market that it effectively bars others from entry. This type of barrier to entry is usually related to capital structure, and it is extremely difficult to move far in this direction alone before losing ground to one's peers who have chosen not to take on greater capital responsibilities.

Over time, the only way to improve pricing flexibility is to move northeastward *as an industry*. Simultaneous movement on both axes gives improved capitalization with the protection of higher public perception to drive service demand. Unfortunately, this strategy demands success at two of the very things that nonprofit organizations as a whole have not been good at in the past: acting in concert and self-policing.

Acting in concert means giving up a bit of autonomy in return for advancement of the field. For a variety of reasons, the normal mode of operation for nonprofits has been much more of an independent style. That kind of genteel anarchy may benefit individual players, but it does nothing for the whole. Trade groups, professional societies, and nonprofit leaders themselves are the only ones who can boost public perception of value.

Lastly, nonprofits must do a better job of policing themselves. There are rarely any systematic mechanisms in place to insure that sub-par performers will exit the field. Consequently, the public is justified in evaluating a given field at its lowest common denominator. Take child care, for example. Were the average parent to feel that there are solid quality-insuring systems in place such as meaningful licensing, employee selection, worker training, and strict disciplinary codes, he or she would feel somewhat less ambivalent than they typically do now about leaving a child in a professional day care center, and this greater assurance would be reflected in the price.

Critics will say that such an effort is unrealistic since it would involve working with proprietary day care centers as well as nonprofit organizations, and that in any case it would be more expensive than the average family is willing to pay. That is precisely the point: Nonprofits and for-profits must work together to raise the perception of value for both, or else they will fail working apart. And as to price, in most cities, it currently costs more to house a dog for a day in a kennel than it costs to keep a child in day care. There's plenty of room for upside price flexibility.

CHAPTER TWELVE

Profit: Why and How Much?

A chapter on profitability in nonprofit organizations may seem quixotic, but only because there is an unspoken understanding that we never discuss the subject in public. It doesn't help that the term "nonprofit" seems to settle the matter before it's even raised. The result: Those connected with nonprofit organizations—consumers, funders, regulators, and even some managers—have no vocabulary and no common understanding about this financial need that practically cries out for careful attention and management.

This is unfortunate. Profit is part of any organization's economics. The question of who shares in the profit, which is what distinguishes nonprofit organizations from for-profit ones, is really only the last and most uninteresting aspect. Much more important is how it is generated, why, and for what it is used. The lack of frank attention to the subject is what causes us to possess such little collective knowledge of it. The purpose of this chapter is to explain why nonprofit organizations can and would want to earn a profit each year and to suggest ways of making one. 💾

PROFIT DEFINED

First, a definition of profit. For our purposes, we will consider profit to be an excess of revenue over expenses during any given fiscal period. As shown earlier, profit will land on the balance sheet as an increase in a nonprofit's fund balance, offset by an increase in some asset or mix of assets. This dynamic is extremely significant in appreciating the role profit can play in a nonprofit. Remember for a moment that the balance sheet really sketches the financial boundaries of the organization. The larger these boundaries, the larger the organization. Besides profit, there are only two ways to grow the balance sheet. One way is to borrow long-term funding (such as a mortgage) which pushes up the long-term debt line on the liability side of the balance sheet and the cash or building/equipment line on the asset side. The other way to boost the financial dimensions of *any* type of corporation is to get an outsider to give money directly to it. In the proprietary world, this kind of money is given with the quid pro quo of ownership. Whether the money is given in identical small increments by the general public (stocks) or as an individual pumping a large chunk of funds into the organization doesn't matter. Either way, the source of the funds gets a piece of the corporation in return.

Since nonprofit organizations cannot have individual shareholders, this method of raising funds is off limits. The nonprofit counterpart is grants. The only way to get money into a nonprofit corporation with no explicit expectation of the kind of financial return obtainable from borrowing is through fund-raising. A philanthropic term for that strategy is the capital campaign, designed to raise a set amount of money—or capital—in a fixed period of time. In a way, the capital campaign is the equivalent of a stock offering of a for-profit company: A major, orchestrated attempt to sell all or part of the organization to the general public. The difference is that major donors, unlike major stockholders, can get no promise of control or direct economic value in exchange for their money. Any benefits they do receive, such as public recognition, may in fact have value, but it is incidental to the transaction.

These simple facts create a serious structural blockage to adequate capitalization in a nonprofit corporation. If selling shares in the entity is forbidden and if a capital campaign is unrealistic, as it is for many nonprofits, there will be extra pressure on the two remaining ways of bringing in capital, borrowing and profits.

USES OF PROFIT

Internally generated profits are the major capital source under the routine control of the nonprofit manager. There is no practical alternative. This puts enormous pressure on the organization's internal management controls to produce a surplus on a regular basis, while simultaneously negotiating the kind of political crosscurrents around the profitability issue that will be covered later in this chapter. The pivotal question is how much profit is "enough."

Fortunately, that question now becomes easier to answer. The question of how much profit is enough is intimately linked to the uses to which that profit will be put. To no one's surprise, the uses of profit in a nonprofit corporation are exactly the same as those in a proprietary organization, save for the transfer of wealth to the owner.

First, an explanatory note: The following material—and the formulas themselves—are intended as planning guides rather than as inviolable rules. Their ultimate purpose is to stimulate careful consideration of the uses of profit in nonprofit corporations. Since the uses of profit are unrelated to each other, it is possible to plan for more than one during the same budget period. In that case, the percentages suggested should be regarded as building blocks of the eventual projected profit margin. In any event, these constructs can operate as guiding frameworks for planning and evaluating profitability.

Profit for Stability

Stability is probably the most common and easily understood use for profits in a nonprofit. For a corporation with adequate and reliable funding and good systems, stability created by profitability can mean the ability to concentrate on mission without energy-draining fiscal distractions. A year or two of solid profitability for a nonprofit in crisis can mean that meeting the payroll will become a routine possibility instead of a weekly crisis.

Stability is the holy grail of nonprofit management. It is the desirable financial characteristic most often referred to by nonprofit employees, boards of directors, and management itself. It is also harder to achieve in a nonprofit setting than in a for-profit one, if for no other reason than that the nonprofit's financial bullseye is smaller. Miss the target profit goal in a proprietary entity and you still have a chance to break even. Miss breakeven in a nonprofit and you inescapably lose money.

As an operating guide, the notion of stability is a fuzzy thing. Probe deeply enough and you are likely to get numerous indicators of a state of financial stability. Still, there are probably a few shared themes. Stability is the absence of unpleasant surprises. For those working in an organization, the chief unpleasant surprise is certainly a missed paycheck. Another unpleasant surprise is the overall crunch caused by a large unexpected expense, even if it does not cause a missed payroll. Beyond these, the problems typically encountered in the ordinary course of events ought to be able to be handled by an organization with an ordinarily balanced state of financial health. (See Chapter Four on diagnostic tools for some insights into what this might look like. *Caution:* It will be different for different organizations.)

If stability for the majority of people in a nonprofit essentially means no missed payrolls and no general feeling of financial pressure, then stability for practicing managers translates into keeping enough cash on hand. Equipped with this insight, we can build a serviceable answer to the question, "How much profit is enough to maintain stability?"

What follows is intended only as a rough planning guide, not a precise formula for action. But first, we need to make a few assumptions:

- The rest of the organization is in a more or less steady state, even if that state is not entirely satisfactory to its managers. Therefore, what we will be calculating is an amount over and above existing levels of liquidity.

- The funds generated for stability will go directly to cash and not be diverted to other expenses, such as covering an increase in accounts receivable or to purchase a building. If this does happen, of course, the cash needed to cover these activities must be generated independently from our profit-for-stability calculation.

- These are one-year estimates only; at some point, the desirable level of cash will materialize, and when it does there will be no more need to generate profits solely to achieve stability.

The formula for profit-for-stability is:

$$P/E \times A$$

Where P = Total annual personnel costs, including payroll taxes
   and fringe benefits
  E = Total annual expenses
  A = Amount of one payroll period expressed as a
   percentage of annual payroll (Assumes one payroll
   period beyond the current one is sufficient to be ahead;
   double it if two payroll periods are desirable instead.)

As an example, suppose an organization spends $7.5 million of its $10 million total budget on personnel-related expenses and wants to be one week ahead of its weekly payroll. Its formula for profit-for-stability would be:

$$\frac{7,500,000}{10,000,000} \times .019 = 1.4\% \text{ Profit margin}$$

Again, it is important to stress that this number is for rough planning purposes only, and that in order for it to adequately bolster the cash position, all other sources and uses of cash must cancel each other out for the period.

Profit for Personnel Bonuses

Another use for profit in a nonprofit is as bonuses for staff. The degree to which this is surprising to any given reader is probably the degree to which he or she has been removed from the daily realities of nonprofit administration for the last several years. Not that the practice is limited to nonprofits. Increasingly, American employers of all kinds are turning to some form of incentive-based compensation in lieu of all or part of the yearly merit increase. If anything, nonprofit employers have been a bit slow to adopt the practice.

The economic uncertainties of the early 1990s are subtly beginning to change the use of bonuses. Whereas previously a bonus was regarded as something of a human resource management tool—a reward for good work—now it is often used as a means of giving raises that do not automatically carry into the next year. Consequently, its nature has begun to change from motivational to fiscal. To the extent that this trend takes away some of the emotional context of bonuses, it will make managers' jobs less complicated. The bonus will simply become something akin to delayed compensation with no implied judgment about performance.

The way profit is used for bonuses in nonprofits usually involves budgeting on the basis of unchanged or minimally changed salaries and wages from the previous year. Then, approximately nine or ten months into the fiscal year, the executive director and business manager (or their equivalent departments) take stock of the financial situation and decide whether or not they can afford to give bonuses this year. If they decide to give bonuses, it will typically be done at the end of the fiscal year and be labeled "one-time wage adjustment" or some other innocuous sounding phrase—anything but the term "bonus."

There is nothing illegal about this practice, although the bookkeeping and linguistic contortions managers often go through do raise the aura of ethical concerns for some. In part this is due to the still-prevalent notion that those who work in a nonprofit organization of any kind must be motivated by the pleasures of the work itself and not by money. At the same time, there is an underlying legal issue related to incentive-based compensation in a tax-exempt sphere that deserves a full explanation.

The legal issue in question is the doctrine of *private inurement,* which is strictly prohibited by federal law. Private inurement at its simplest means that the owners of an organization export all or part of the profits of that organization into their own coffers. In the case of publicly held corporations, this occurs when stockholders vote themselves a dividend. It is not only legal; it is the very reason for the company's existence.

There is no direct parallel in nonprofit corporations because it simply is not allowed; wealth or profits created by a nonprofit must stay in the organization and not flow into private owners' pockets. Since nonprofits cannot have stockholders, there is no distribution mechanism in place to get wealth out of the organization into private hands. However, there is an extremely common mechanism for drawing certain funds from a nonprofit and putting them into private hands. It is called the payroll, and this is why the most typical form of private inurement in a nonprofit setting is excessive or unreasonable compensation to an insider who has at least some control over the payment of that benefit (i.e., director, officer, trustee, substantial benefactor, family member, key staff person).

The role of compensation as a potential fiscal sluiceway out of the nonprofit corporation is what worries authorities. Still, as Bruce Hopkins points out with a quote from the U.S. Tax Court, "[t]he law places no duty on individuals operating charitable organizations to donate their services; they are entitled to reasonable compensation for their services." Consequently, painting any given compensation arrangement with an insider as a form of private inurement is an intrinsically tricky business.

Ultimately, the courts seem to hold excessive compensation as a form of private inurement when either it is high in absolute terms or when the inurement is calculated with no natural cap in mind. Each case is decided individually, however, and there are enough subtle nuances in the decisions that have been rendered to make most knowledgeable attorneys balk at the idea of declaring a particular arrangement acceptable or not without a court test.

The upshot of all this is that it leaves nonprofit boards and managers a great deal of latitude in determining incentive-based compensation. One thing that is certain is that they have far more discretion than most believe. For example, a commission-based system alone is not considered evidence of private inurement. Paying bonuses, in other words, does not endanger a nonprofit's tax-exempt status. Funding sources may not like it, but that is a different issue. In practice, we can reasonably expect more and more nonprofits to adopt incentive-based compensation in the coming years as economic conditions virtually demand it.

Happily then, it is permissible to use profit for staff bonuses as long as the program is properly structured. Having said this, we are once again left with the question of how much. The question is answerable only in the aggregate since what we can create is a bonus pool for distribution according to some specially constructed formulas. This time the calculation is a bit simpler than profit for stability. Profit for bonuses is:

$$\frac{S}{E} \times B$$

Where S = Total annual salaries paid to employees eligible for bonus

E = Total annual expenses

B = Amount of average bonus, expressed as a percentage

For example, if a nonprofit with total salaries of $300,000 and total annual expenses of $500,000 sought a bonus pool of 3 percent of the actual margin, they should plan for $9,000, as follows:

$$\frac{\$300,000}{\$500,000} \times 0.03 = 0.6 \times 0.03$$
$$= 1.8\% \times \$500,000$$
$$= \$9,000$$

It seems only fair to use profits for personnel bonuses since it is spending on personnel that usually yields the greatest savings, as explained later. These calculations are useful as a guide to planning for profits, or as an after-the-fact guide to using profits created.

Profit for Innovation

Using profits for innovation or research and development is a new concept for some nonprofits because there is usually no incentive for a nonprofit to innovate. Unlike a for-profit company for whom any kind of innovation can translate into increased market share which can translate into turbocharged profits, the nonprofit's only motivation for being innovative derives from intangibles such as desire, dedication, or an individual's sheer ego gratification.

Never underestimate the importance of the latter motivation. Some of the most influential and entrepreneurial nonprofits in the country have been built through the force of a single individual's will. A subset of this kind of drive—and a far more common kind than one might imagine—is the will to create a nonprofit organization for ideological reasons. Whole organizations, even entire nonprofit industries, have been created in order to further agendas as diverse as noninstitutional care for the mentally retarded, specific religious beliefs, and environment-centered activities.

The larger context is one of values. Starting with nonprofits' historic roots in religious action, a great many nonprofit organizations have been unique value systems engaged to accomplish a specific purpose. In effect, the currency of a nonprofit organization is not money but values. This is why the output of many nonprofits is so hard to quantify. Output is a secondary consideration. To varying degrees of explicitness, conflict in a nonprofit will center around the evolution of the value system.

In truth, much of the innovative thinking goes on before the nonprofit entity is even established. Paradoxically, it is precisely when a nonprofit organization is innovative that it has the best chance of advancing its own values. Proponents of community-based mental health and mental retardation conceived of treatment in the least restrictive environment possible, thereby revolutionizing an entire system of care. Community economic development agencies typically feel a passionate commitment to giving poor people greater power over their own housing and employment decisions.

In the twenty-first century, the pressure will be on nonprofits to innovate. Until the 1990s, nonprofits generally had been buffered from the effects of innovation typical of industry because it normally occurred in areas of technology or middle management, neither of which most nonprofit organizations use in abundance. However, in the future, the pressure to innovate will come to direct services (in some areas, it already has), and the intelligent nonprofit will be prepared.

A planned profit to support innovation is difficult to calculate for many reasons, including the fact that it may be a bit arbitrary to draw a line around a certain group of expenses and pronounce them innovation expenses. To the extent that an innovation effort requires new and easily identifiable expenses—like salaries or the purchase of equipment—its formula would look like this:

$$\frac{I}{CE}$$

Where I   = Amount of cash required yearly for innovation
              purposes
        CE = Yearly cash expenses

So if a nonprofit needed an annual cash outlay of $80,000 for, say, salaries and direct expenses related to a new way it was developing to secure financing for low-income homebuyers and its annual cash expenses were $4,000,000, it would need to set aside 2 percent of its annual budget as profit.

Profit for Growth

Finally, profit can play a supporting role in what we'll call growth. In some ways, this is a catch-all category composed of the elements defined above, but in a much broader sense, growth in a financial context means growth in revenues and probably in the accompanying balance sheet, although it will come in different ways. For example, growth in some fields necessitates carrying more accounts receivable. At the least, growth in any field means having enough cash available to seize opportunities or cushion unexpected losses. Generating profits can help tremendously.

Due to the wide-open nature of financial growth and what it could mean to any given organization, there really is no formula available to assist with planning. Since growth can take an infinite variety of forms and dimensions, there is no alternative but to look at each situation individually and make an estimate of what is necessary in order to translate it into a profit planning percentage.

A final word of clarification for those of you who object to defining growth exclusively in financial terms—you're right. Growth in a nonprofit whose mission is to serve the public means something fundamentally different than growth in a proprietary company. Action for Children's Television, a semi-legendary nonprofit dedicated to reforming television programming targeting children, never grew much in a financial sense at all. Its growth was entirely programmatic and political in nature, as it came to be seen for many years as the dominant credible voice in the campaign to reform commercial television having children as the market.

Still, for many if not most organizations, growth in ability to accomplish a mission usually entails growth in a financial sense, too. In fact, for many types of public service, the two are inseparable: Growth in the financial dimension should be seen not as the byproduct but as the necessary precondition to growth in mission.

PROFIT—HOW TO GET IT

Nowhere in nonprofit management matters is there a starker division between what is financially desirable and what is politically possible than in the question of how to generate profits. For all our talk otherwise, we as a society show a curious ambivalence about profits in the for-profit world. Rarely does a proprietary concern deal explicitly with something called profit. Instead, profit gets taken out of an entity in the form of high salaries, or it is buried in a mixed category loosely called "overhead," or owners receive "distributions."

We see the same aversion to the idea of profit in the nonprofit sector, except that it is magnified many times over and generates downright hostility. The unspoken message is that a dollar of profit in a nonprofit means a dollar less of services provided. To make matters more complicated, this is true in extreme cases. Then again, it is the extreme cases that the IRS has the power to discipline, leaving the ordinary nonprofit and its management at the mercy of conventional thinking.

What can correct for this tendency is the practical nonprofit executive's or board's realization that constant losses drain the organization instead of ennobling it. Those who understand this contradiction then enter into a kind of schizoid existence in which they must appear to support the conventional thinking with the one hand while with the other they frantically attempt to create profits. Or, to be more precise, they attempt to create situations in which profits can seem to arise, unbidden and unexpected.

This forced serendipity is crazy. It requires managers to pretend that they are interested in keeping the original budget on track when what they really want to do is shave a bit from it. Those unaware of the riddle see management making apparently senseless decisions and holding back on perfectly reasonable and already justified expenditures.

The unacknowledged game has two major negative impacts on nonprofit organizations. First, lack of profitability means putting the corporation on an endlessly regressive spiral, always looking to cut back and forego rather than to build. The fact that nonprofit groups of all kinds tend to have fixed revenues—either by funding source design or by management's failure to value growth—compounds the inherent need to look to spending reductions for profit. Second, employees are affected. When managers must look for reductions in expenses to create profit, certain spending is exempt. For instance, some occupancy costs, especially leases or mortgages, are inescapable. Other expenses may be flexible within only narrow limits. At any rate, these costs of doing business pale in comparison to the largest and most flexible source of savings of them all—spending on personnel. Most nonprofit organizations spend 60 percent to 80 percent of their budgets on personnel, so it is inevitable that personnel spending gets a lot of attention when the search is on for savings.

Because of this, nonprofit staff often feel under siege and vulnerable. Even if the ultimate use for some of the savings is bonuses, the process of culling the money to fund bonuses from the personnel budget can be a brutal one. Frequently it requires future staff to give up resources equivalent to present staff's bonuses. Techniques for causing this shift range from deliberately delaying replacement of departing staff to not hiring for a planned position at all. Still, if everyone understands the reasons for personnel decisions like these, it lays the groundwork for success.

WHAT CAN BE DONE

For-profit corporations do not need to think twice about the role of profit in their organizations; nonprofit organizations do. Since the resources of a nonprofit corporation cannot be transferred into private hands except through the conventional (and more regulated) means of salary and benefits, the question of profit planning becomes one of timing and balance. The nonprofit executive is forever balancing the short-term demands of personnel and suppliers against the long-term financial needs of the entity. Because the resources must remain in the organization no matter what, the debate is over where they will be used.

There is perhaps no better way to prepare for a given level of profit than an informed, organization-wide discussion of the issue. Not that all employees need to become amateur financial managers. Instead, there needs to be widespread understanding and acceptance of the need for profit as an integral part of nonprofit corporate financial health. There need not be great tension around fiscal decisions regarding profit if the realities of nonprofit finance are understood by all key players.

PART FOUR

Control

CHAPTER THIRTEEN

Internal Controls for External Goals

When the talk turns to the subject of Mildred the controller, her boss grows effusive:

Mildred is a treasure. We call her our controller but she's really so much more. She's the first one in the office every morning and usually the last one to leave. She never takes a vacation. Last year I practically ordered her to take a week off and she couldn't do it—she came back two days early. Said she was worried about the new payroll system. She's been around for almost fifteen years now, longer than any of the rest of us, and she knows everything about this office. Never afraid to pitch in and do someone else's job temporarily. I don't know where we'd be without Mildred.

Probably several thousand dollars a year richer. You see, Mildred is an embezzler. This is the portrait of a quiet crook. She works those long hours to keep an eye on everyone else. The reason she can't take a vacation is that if her system is left unattended for any period of time it may collapse. She wasn't worried about the new payroll system, either, she just needed to make sure it didn't accidentally uncover one of her schemes. Sure she'll pitch in to do someone else's job. It keeps her on top of everyone and everything in the office.

Now before you complain that I am picking on old ladies, I never said she was old. Actually, she could be only 33, having started with the agency as a high school student, or she could be middle-aged, or her name could be Lawrence, who's not a treasure at all but a surly bookkeeper of indeterminate age and questionable competence. Or Lawrence might not be a bookkeeper, but rather an executive director who routinely makes colossal errors in financial management.

You get the point. A threat to a nonprofit's financial health looks like Mildred . . . or Lawrence . . . or like you or me. In fact, there is no one portrait of an internal financial threat, no single characteristic that they all have in common. Fraud, error, and bad management operate in a multitude of different ways, and it is the nonprofit corporation's responsibility to prevent or minimize the possible damage. Preventing loss of resources by making errors less likely and fraud more easily detected is the job of the system of internal controls.

THE ELEMENTS OF INTERNAL CONTROL

The problem with the concept of internal controls is not that they are vague, but that the phrase encompasses such a wide range of conditions, actions, and systems. Six important elements of an internal control system are:

1. Control cues
2. Policy communication
3. Segregation of duties
4. Recordkeeping
5. Budgets
6. Reporting.

Taken together, these policies sketch the acceptable boundaries for fiscal decisions, govern the way resources are allocated, provide information for evaluation, and define the processes that are to be used in carrying out the organization's mission. In short, they control the organization. We'll take each one in order except for budgets, which was covered in detail in Chapter Ten "Taming the Budget Beast."

Control Cues

Strangely enough, the most efficient means of controlling the non-profit organization is the cheapest. I call these collected communications "control cues." They are the signals that management and board send about the safeguarding of assets and accurate financial reporting. No matter what the content, these activities put out stronger messages about what managers value and the level of accountability they demand than all of the computer software or policy memoranda combined.

The reason that control cues are cheap is that they are largely symbolic. Frequently, they consist mostly of not doing things. The executive director does not put her personal mail in the outgoing mail pile to be run through the agency's postage meter: the business manager doesn't leave the door to the safe wide open the whole day even if it is more convenient that way. On a more substantive level, managers in the adequately controlled nonprofit corporation communicate their expectations of proper control and train staff at all levels in matters of control policies appropriate to them. For example, management letters from yearly audits frequently mention systemic breakdowns in internal controls: these should be corrected as quickly as possible. Appropriate security should be designed and maintained for all computerized records, and so on. Over time, dozens of small cues add up to an overall picture of control and accountability that tend to discourage people from even trying anything underhanded.

Policy Communication

The challenge for the designer of a communication system is to do it as efficiently yet as thoroughly as possible. The stakes are high since a large measure of accountability to external forces derives from how transactions are handled internally. On the other hand, this is one of those areas where reality has outpaced theory. One of the easiest suggestions an outsider such as an auditor can make about a system of internal controls is that it needs a written policy and procedures manual. Unhappily, it usually doesn't happen that way. The next time that the business staff of the average small- to medium-sized nonprofit organization has the time to sit down and carefully document its internal control policies and procedures in a three-ring binder with tabs will be the first time. Larger nonprofits have to maintain some form of internal control manual in order to simply survive, but it is remarkable how often the official documentation is lacking or out of date.

The fact is that few nonprofit corporations actually maintain such policies and procedures manuals, and yet many have as good a system of internal controls as one could wish. The reason is that they have an effective system of communication about changes in policies and procedures, it just doesn't happen to take the form of a manual. Improvements in communication technology over the past few years have helped a lot in this regard, as have organizational changes that the technology has facilitated. The fact that many nonprofits have small business office staffs doesn't hurt either, since they are better able to communicate with each other without layers of bureaucracy.

Today, technology such as computer networks, voice mail, and fax machines can accommodate an organization's need to communicate widely while remaining highly flexible. The real challenge is to make use of each form of communication while keeping the content coherent and retrievable. The three-ring binder with carefully typed tabs specifying all aspects of the accounting system may be history, but the need for communication will always be with us.

Segregation of Duties

Think of an accounting system as a series of vulnerable areas or pressure points susceptible to leakage and distortion of results. These points are natural and inevitable, and they represent the areas where breakdowns in control are most likely to occur. It is not inappropriate to think about an accounting system as though it were under permanent siege by forces that would corrupt its processes and divert its assets. The analogy to a castle is tempting except that, unlike a castle, an accounting system is endangered far more by those from within than by those from without.

Embezzlement is a loner's crime. Robbing banks takes gangs, but gangs in a back room are hard to put together and even harder to maintain. Thievery from the ledger requires patience and a certain amount of planning, and the best way to keep it going is to wholly dominate a segment of business operations. The point of internal controls is to insert a system of checks and balances that make that domination harder and to increase the likelihood of detection should it occur.

Inside financial crimes tend to be unoriginal. There is very little new for fiscal bad guys. Sophisticated computer capability sometimes makes the crook's job easier and faster, but the broad outlines have stayed the same. In the end, unauthorized entry is unauthorized entry whether it occurs in a safe or a computerized bank file.

One of the easiest and cheapest ways to thwart those bent on financial crime is to break up the various duties so as to make it nearly impossible for any one person to gain the kind of total dominance over a portion of the system mentioned earlier. This segregating of financial duties creates a network of safeguards at the various pressure points that makes it much more difficult to coordinate and expand fraudulent activity or to accidentally lose assets. It is still possible for a determined embezzler to steal from the nonprofit via even a single pressure point, and human error can play terrible tricks on the strongest of systems. As a result, the siege of internal controls has to be vigorously maintained and routinely updated to take into account new developments in the nonprofit's financial life.

There are any number of potential weak spots in an accounting system. Fortunately, for each one there are one or more things that the careful manager can do to minimize the risk. Preventing loss is a lot easier and less expensive than coping with it, so here are some not-so-rare scenarios along with tips on preventing them at the end of each segment.

▶ Opening the Mail, Receiving Cash

Sure, I realize that opening the mail is not the most exciting job. But I don't mind. This is an old, established, excruciatingly wonderful organization that gets lots of support from lots of different people. I see big foundation checks rolling in from time to time, and some money from the government. But what I really like are the contributions.

Like this one, for example. Handwritten envelope. Shaky writing—probably someone older and not inclined to make trouble. I slit open the envelope and spot a ten dollar bill. I slide it under some papers on my desk. It'll go into my wallet later today. It's only ten dollars, they'll never feel it. They never send thank you notes, so the donor won't know it's gone. Besides, if they ever ask me about it, I'll just lie. Do it again in a week or so, maybe for a bigger amount then.

A few years ago they also let me receive cash for the agency. I made a lot of mistakes at first, and then I realized that an intentional mistake now and then can accomplish as much as an accidental one. I know opening the mail and accepting cash is pretty boring stuff but I don't mind . . .

Prevention

Recruit and hire employees with a focus on proven honesty. Train staff in proper techniques of handling cash and recording donations. Replace any long time mail handler at least temporarily and monitor cash intake to see if it changes. Use an imprest fund for petty cash, meaning a locked box (with only two or three authorized key holders) always containing the same amount of money in some combination of cash and receipts; for example, if I take out ten dollars in cash, I must replace it with ten dollars in receipts. Use prenumbered receipts and monitor their usage. Restrictively endorse checks upon receipt and list cash received. Use a lockbox for collections (a service offered by a bank in which donors or payment sources send money directly to a bank's post office box number). Bond—take out a specialized type of insurance—any employee handling cash or other assets.

◀

▶ Who Mails?

I hope they give me the job of sending out the mail. Boy, would that make my scam easier. It would be a lot nicer to know when those payments for the fake invoices were going out. Better control, you understand.

Prevention

Be sure that the person who mails is not the same person who writes the checks and signs them.

◀

▶ Writing and Signing Checks

My name is Doris, and I hold the pen—the check writing pen, that is. Vendors and suppliers who want the corporation to transfer some of its assets to them to satisfy an outstanding bill have to go through me. They don't see me. In most cases, they don't even talk with me. That's all right, because I don't need them. I have my own suppliers that I like to do business with. One of them has an office address that's a vacant lot. Another has been out of business for three years. A third is a figment of my imagination. All of them exist for the same reason—to help me trick this nonprofit corporation into writing checks to people who shouldn't be receiving them. Like me, for instance.

The process of check issuance has three steps: authorizing a check to be cut, creating the check, and signing it. I cover two of the three. Over the years, they gave me the power to authorize certain checks, mainly administrative and occupancy-related supplies. Since I also write out most of our nonpayroll checks, I only need to worry about getting the bogus checks signed. That turns out to be pretty simple. Watch.

I have to get this batch of checks signed by the executive director. I bury the bogus one in the middle of the pile and walk into her office when I know she'll be on the phone. I see her talking and pretend to look flustered. She smiles, motions to me to come on in. "Uh huh, uh huh. Sure," she's saying into the phone as I lay the pile of checks in front of her. She scribbles her signature furiously on one check after another. She bought a special cradle for the telephone receiver to balance it on her shoulder precisely for moments like this one (I ordered it for her). "I couldn't agree with you more," she's saying, "but we have to get Matt to sign off on it."

Boom. Done. The check to my weed lot is signed and ready to be deposited in my special account. Nobody is going to ask for it back, and I am going to quietly remove key documentation so that it's not clear what prompted the false payment in the first place (it was my false invoice). The odds against the auditors selecting that check or vendor for testing are slim, so I have probably gotten away with a few thousand dollars no one will ever find.

Prevention

Different people should be responsible for each of the three steps involved in writing a check. Have the manager closest to the service that caused the expense initial each invoice prior to payment. Never let the person writing the check be the person signing. Insure a system of formal as well as informal communication between the direct service aspect of the organization and the administrative support function. Require highest check signing authority for the largest checks. Give managers information on their departments' spending patterns and research results that one or both of you cannot easily explain. Make sure check signers pay attention to what they are signing. Occasionally, pick checks at random and work backward to their point of origin. Check signers insure that checks are mailed in a timely fashion and in the way intended. Educate staff at all levels in the meaning and implications of related party transactions (financial transactions between the nonprofit and someone connected with it such as a board member, officer, etc.).

▶ Approve Payroll

I'm not going to tell you my name since that would blow my cover. Let's just say that I don't have to work real hard for my paycheck. In fact, I don't even have to work at all. Don't get me wrong—my paperwork is in order, and the bookkeeping office thinks I'm just one of hundreds of hard working stiffs in this nonprofit. As far as all the records are concerned, I'm golden. It's just that I don't have to do anything to get paid.

I am part of a small office several miles from the central office headquarters. They say we're outstationed to another nonprofit's programs in the building, which really means nobody knows what we're doing except that we're doing it outside of the normal central office and program locations. It started a few years ago when this organization took over a group of scattered programs with lousy administrative systems. I have a cousin who is pretty influential around town and apparently someone owed him something. Nobody figured out what was going on then, and as long as nobody from this business office talks to anyone at the program they probably never will . . .

Prevention

All supervisors must have full knowledge at all times of staff, their salaries, and work expectations. A position control system backs up this level of knowledge by specifying authorized levels of staffing, budgeted amounts, and details of the actual staffing complement. A position control system is practically mandatory for any nonprofit employing hundreds of employees. It can be as simple as a computerized spreadsheet or as elaborate as a module in an accounting system. Plain communication helps, too. Business staff and direct service staff need multiple opportunities to communicate, and a framework for identifying and researching unexplained variances from budget. Middle managers in charge of programs need to know exactly what personnel they have been allocated and why, and they should be held accountable for how they use them.

◀

▶ Creating Financial Records

Me, I like detail. The more the better. I especially like details like how a transaction gets entered in our books, and the amounts recorded on bank deposit slips. You can call me Albert or Randall, if you prefer. I also answer to Charles and, of course, John. These are all my friends, and during the course of a year most of them turn up in our financial records. Sometimes they have checks made out to them or their companies, and other times they just appear in our records to cover some other deal I'm working.

None of my friends are real, you see. Instead, I think of each one as extensions of my personality. I am an artist, you might say, a creator of financial fictions, and this nonprofit's books are my canvas. It helps that I have responsibility for entering lots of transactions as they occur, and for reconciling the records with our bank accounts. Keeps me in control of the loop, and everybody else outside of it.

Prevention

Separate bank statement reconciliation from the completion of deposit slips. Separate the processing functions such as receiving and preparing for recording a transaction from the actual recording of it. Require approval for interfund transfers.

◀

Making Segregation of Duties Work in a Nonprofit Setting.
There are many other duties whose components can be segregated
in the typical nonprofit organization. For instance, custody of securities is a major issue for nonprofits fortunate enough to own
some and is one reason why portfolio management is best en-
trusted to professional money managers. There will also be many
other duties unique to a nonprofit organization that will need to
be split up in order to help insure adequate control. Still, this is a
book for those who rely on systems of segregation of duties, not for
those who must create them. The power of segregating duties is
clear, and the wise manager will use it carefully.

The real obstacle to effective segregation of duties in a nonprofit
setting is not so much lack of knowledge as it is lack of people. A
very rough (emphasis on *very*) rule of thumb is that for nonprofit
organizations with revenues greater than approximately $1 mil-
lion, it should take one to two full-time equivalent (FTE) financial
people plus an additional 0.25 to 1.5 FTE per million dollars of revenue thereafter, with the rate of additional staff tailing off at the
industry's typical economic size (see Box).

Unfortunately from the perspective of controls, most nonprofit
groups under $1 million in revenue have one or fewer people iden-
tified as financial staff, and it will usually be someone concerned
with keeping the financial records, not managing them.

It is impossible to segregate duties when one person does it all.
In those circumstances, it is necessary for another individual, most
likely the executive director, to take on complementary control duties. Happily, it is possible to achieve a reasonable degree of segregation even with two people. With more people, it becomes that
much easier. *The Nonprofit Management Reports* (Third Sector Press)
developed a very useful set of sample duty allocations for two-,
three-, and four-person offices. These are reproduced in Exhibit
13.1. A matrix for pinpointing weaknesses in internal control is in
the diskette.

Recordkeeping

The actual pathways of information flow are contained in the financial recordkeeping systems the nonprofit maintains. In principle, a recording system is pretty simple. It keeps track of money

Economic Size

The consistent inability to handle routine administrative tasks may be a signal that a nonprofit is operating below its field's desirable economic size.

Some nonprofits cannot afford to have the level of business expertise on staff that they really need. While one reason is the chronic underfunding of administration by funding sources and some managers themselves, another reason may be that the nonprofit is not of a sufficient economic size.

In order to open its doors, any nonprofit must invest in a fixed amount of administrative equipment and personnel. In most cases, this implies computers, telephone systems, an office, and personnel. Most nonprofits allocate a small percentage of each incoming revenue dollar to meet these needs. More sophisticated and varied demands on the financial and administrative systems mean higher fixed costs.

If those financial and administrative needs are costly—if, for instance, the nonprofit requires complex software and high-level accounting personnel—the only way to get those things if the allocation percentage stays the same is to increase the number of revenue dollars. At the point where there is a reasonable balance between the amount of programming delivered and the adequacy of the financial and administrative systems is the economic size.

We know what happens if the nonprofit is below the economic size—it will be unable to perform properly and with financial accountability. What we don't know for most fields in which nonprofits are active is whether it is possible to miss the economic size by being too large. Much more research is needed here.

coming into and money flowing out of the organization, and it makes sure that all documentation of the flow is summarized in the general ledger. In practice, the details can get quite complex, but the underlying principles don't change. Exhibit 13.2 shows the relationships among the various parts of the recordkeeping system.

Two-Person Segregation

Business Manager	CEO
Post accounts receivable	Sign checks
Mail checks	Sign employee contracts
Write checks	Custody of securities
Post general ledger	Complete deposit slips
Reconcile bank statements	Perform interfund transfers
Post credits/debits	Distribute payroll
Give credits and discounts	Reconcile petty cash
Approve payroll	Record initial charge/pledge
Open mail/receive cash	Approve employee time sheets
Disburse petty cash	Prepare invoices
Authorize purchase orders	Complete check log
Authorize check requests	
Authorize invoices for payment	

Three-Person Segregation

Bookkeeper	Business Manager	CEO
Post accounts receivable	Prepare invoices	Sign checks
Reconcile petty cash	Record initial charge/pledge	Sign employee contracts
Write checks	Open mail/receive cash	Custody of securities
Post general ledger	Mail checks	Complete deposit slips
Reconcile bank statements	Approve invoices for payment	Perform interfund transfers
Post credits/debits	Distribute payroll	
Gives credits and discounts	Authorize purchase orders	
	Authorize check requests	
	Approve employee time sheets	
	Approve payroll	
	Complete check log	
	Disburse petty cash	

Exhibit 13.1   Segregation of Duties

Four-Person Segregation			
Bookkeeper	*Clerk*	*Business Manager*	*CEO*
Post accounts receivable	Distribute payroll slips	Complete deposit	Sign checks
Reconcile petty cash	Open mail/receive cash	Give credits and discounts	Sign employee contracts
Write checks	Record initial charges & pledges	Prepare invoices	Custody of securities
Post general ledger	Complete check log	Approve payroll	Approve employee timesheets
Post credits/ debits	Disburse petty cash	Approve invoices for payment	Perform interfund transfers
Reconcile bank statements	Authorize purchase orders		
	Authorize check requests		
	Mail checks		

Exhibit 13.1   Continued

Money Coming In:

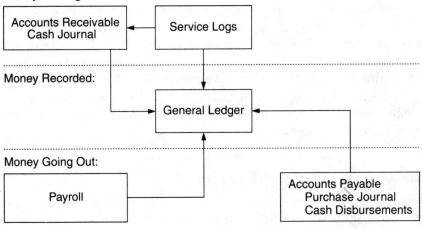

Exhibit 13.2 Sample Recordkeeping System

Czar Nicholas Alexander was said to have sighed on his deathbed, "I never ran Russia; a thousand clerks did." Most nonprofit executive directors feel the same way about the financial operations of their nonprofit. For that matter, so do many financial managers. The recordkeeping system is just that—a system. It is of necessity a gigantic commodity processor, and its commodity is financial transactions. Nobody can be said to run it in the same sense that one runs a piece of heavy equipment or an automobile. At base it is nothing more than small units of information going through proscribed processes in carefully determined steps. The systemic aspect consists of trying to get the same results every time that one starts with the same type of input.

If one were able to turn a financial recordkeeping system into sound, it would probably be like thundershowers on a tin roof.

Just like thundershowers, financial transactions keep coming, the pace intensifying around certain times of the day and periods of the year. There is no respite when overseeing a financial recordkeeping system.

This nonstop pace dictates that each transaction be handled rapidly and accurately or else the entire system bogs down and eventually stops altogether. It also means that the way to judge a system is via whole groups of transactions, not by how well it does on one or two transactions. But there is an ironic twist to evaluating a financial system. A large majority of transactions in any agency of size recur along similar lines, and it is a straightforward matter to compose a system for processing them. Some percentage of transactions, however, are unusual or nonrecurring, and these must be handled quickly and effectively because otherwise the entire system bogs down. It can be said that the mark of a good system is one that can handle volume without being so imprisoned in routine that it cannot cope with variety.

HOW TO MONITOR THE SYSTEM

For the nonprofit executive or manager assigned responsibility for a financial system but despairing of his or her ability to control it, there is a reassuring and effective method of getting the job done. *Let someone else do it.* Seriously, there is a considerable amount of outside help available to perform some of the recordkeeping functions or to help shape how they are performed, and a secondary payoff is that this simplifies the control function. Here, in no particular order of importance, are some of the ways the smart manager can leverage outside help to maintain proper internal controls.

Use a Payroll Service

Thanks to a steady accumulation of laws, regulations, conventional practices, and competitive strategies, preparing any organization's payroll has become an absolute swamp. Just getting the correct withholding amounts for each employee is a challenge in itself, especially with recent changes in calculating withholding amounts. Contracting it out is usually a good idea. In fact, there are only two types of nonprofits that may have a good reason for doing their own payrolls: the very small who can't afford even an extra dime, and the very large that can afford to staff their own internal payroll departments. (Note to the small: Find the dime. Note to the large: Stop kidding yourselves.)

Large national firms now compete to provide payroll services to nonprofit organizations of all kinds. Many banks are also still in the payroll service business, although others have lost their enthusiasm for it. And in every major city, there are local payroll service bureaus catering to a particular niche. Often these bureaus operate independently for some period of years and then are purchased by one of the national firms.

What all of these companies have in common is that they are the ones that deal with the rapidly changing laws, regulations, and schedules that one must master in order to pay American employees correctly today. Due to the nature of the payroll business, they must compete on price and then service. It adds up to good value and reliable accountability for the practicing manager.

Finally, it should be noted that payroll service companies typically offer a wide array of options for using their services, ranging from pick up/drop off services for payroll data and completed check delivery to sophisticated computer linkups between the user and the bureau's computer system. Increasingly, there is little reason for the average nonprofit agency to go it alone in this crucial area.

Accounts Receivable Management

Accounts receivable (A/R) may be another candidate to let outside services manage. Often, when invoices must be prepared according to strict guidelines and the nonprofit expects to submit large numbers of them, the stage is set for outside expertise in the billing process.

Sometimes this expertise is a service that looks like a payroll service bureau. Volume makes it all work, since the billing service can achieve economies of scale. Sometimes it takes the form of specialized software, operated with or without the continued involvement of the billing specialists.

Cash Management Services

Banks are the traditional providers of cash management services, and with the changes in the banking industry and the technology of information processing, there is a dizzying array of cash management tools available to nonprofits. It is possible for a bank to take such a strong role in a nonprofit's cash management that the nonprofit's personnel almost literally never touch cash or make any day-to-day cash management decisions other than to request specific amounts of money for operations.

Suppose consumers mail in their payment to a designated post office box. This is a "lockbox" service, in which the bank opens the envelope and deposits the check into a specially designated account. At the close of business that same day, the account is "swept" clean of cash above a predetermined level, with the excess going to an overnight deposit account paying interest at a market level. Automatically—or upon receipt of a signal from the agency—a certain amount over a designated level is removed from *that* account and placed into a longer term instrument paying higher interest rates. Those funds and others on deposit can be electronically transferred to a field office or other recipient. All of this happens without any substantive staff involvement until transaction records are received for reconciliation. Naturally, these types of arrangements are more suitable for larger organizations, but even smaller groups can take advantage of some of them.

MAINTAINING THE SYSTEM

Once a system of internal controls has been assembled, it must be maintained. Most of the changes in its components will be small— a different person starts generating invoices, someone else covers for an absent cash management accountant and never relinquishes the duty—so it may be hard to spot new breakdowns in internal control. Aside from the most important technique of hiring a qualified accounting professional to oversee the accounting system, there are two things nonprofit managers can do to stay on top of the control environment. One is the yearly management letter, and the other is to structure an effective system of financial reports.

The Management Letter

The fastest and most routinely available route to guidance about improving internal controls should be the corporation's annual management letter. An accompanying piece to the annual audit, the management letter is a potentially excellent source of information about how well the system is operating because it is the system of internal controls that can give the outsider the highest degree of comfort that what management presents is in fact what is truly happening.

Typically, the management letter is written with a bit more candor than can be found in the formal financial statements. The idea is that, although the auditors are supposed to report to the board of directors, the management letter is their opportunity to spell out directly to management the improvements that the auditing team feels can be made. It is the only context in which management, the nonprofit's governors, and qualified outside observers can explicitly discuss the heart of what might be called the accountability infrastructure.

The management letter serves as a kind of punch list for repairs to the financial management system over the next 12 months, so it should be quite explicit and practical. In the nonprofit world, it can also serve as a political document in the sense of mediating between board and staff concerns. The bulk of references in a management letter should originate with the auditors, but on occasion they will include a point raised by staff that would have greater importance when coming from outsiders. Whatever their origins, the real message about management letter points is that they should be dealt with by management, preferably within the next twelve months.

Reporting

Put away the printouts. Trash the memos. Forget about the special reports. You only need five financial reports to control the average nonprofit corporation. Breathtaking advances in information processing technology allow us to create a virtually infinite variety of reports, but for high-level oversight, it's hard to beat the basic five: balance sheet, revenue and expenses, aged accounts receivables, cash flow projection, and utilization reporting.

Most of these reports have already been covered elsewhere in this book and need little or no elaboration. The balance sheet will be unaudited, and it should be delivered monthly. Revenue and expenses should be reported by program on both a budget-to-date and year-to-date basis with some form of index to allow quick location of trouble spots. For instance, the final column in the report could be a percentage variance from budget, or whole dollar differences from budget-to-date figures.

Aged accounts receivables (A/R) reports are essential for any organization that does a substantial amount of billing. Also done monthly, the aged A/R reports show the classes of revenue (or the actual outstanding invoices, if practical) and the amounts of each type outstanding for 30, 60, 90, and more days. Cash-flow projections need to be updated at least quarterly if not more often. (Chapter Eight covers this topic in detail.) Finally, most agencies need some form of utilization reporting. Unlike the other four reports, this information varies greatly according to the services provided. It may be enough for a museum to know how many people paid to attend its summer exhibit, for example, while a health center must have detailed information about the different sources of payment its consumers use. There is little alternative but for each type of nonprofit to develop homegrown utilization reports unless they are stipulated by some funding source or a particular format is routinely accepted in its industry.

CONCLUSION

No one in any business entity likes to lose money through error, waste or fraud, but nonprofits must be doubly cautious because of their fiduciary responsibility. Nonprofit financial and accounting systems have natural weak spots, and the goal of a system of internal controls is to prevent loss, or to maximize the chances of detection if loss does occur. Nonfinancial managers need not get enmeshed in the details of running the system of internal controls, but they do need to see that it is maintained. Knowing the components of internal controls helps, as does knowing where to look for information.

CHAPTER FOURTEEN

Management Controls: Toward Accountability for Performance

We end the book with a glimpse into the future. Conventional ways of thinking say we should close with a safe, straightforward discussion of management controls in the nonprofit environment. We should talk about responsibility centers and cost centers and profit centers and all of those other pieces of financial terminology that serve mainly to complicate the obvious. We will do that. But we need to move beyond conventional thinking in order to position nonprofit institutions to function well in the future, and that challenge is by far the more important one for this final chapter.

Nonprofit organizations reflect the environment in which they were created, and for years the same command-and-control approach that won wars, mass-produced billions of dollars worth of consumer goods, and built millions of housing units in this country and around the world served the industrialized world's nonprofits quite well. Management controls were the linchpin that made it all work. Managers exerted their influence on a nonprofit through a system of explicit controls, and the organization moved forward in a linear fashion. Things didn't change much, and when they did, it was usually in a reasonably predictable fashion with plenty of notice. Nonprofit financial management systems were essentially an afterthought, designed with a minimalist's brush and expected to run to keep up with programs' evolution.

MANAGEMENT CONTROLS CIRCA 1980

The conventional formula for management control pivots around the idea of responsibility. Certain points on the organization chart are designated as responsibility centers, meaning that whoever is in charge of that point must either produce something or make something happen. Typically, those in charge are given responsibility for producing profits ("Profit Center"), controlling costs ("Cost Center"), or generating revenue ("Revenue Center"). If circumstances warrant, a fourth category for managing investments might also be added (or it might be considered a profit center). Different organizations may use different language to define these functions, but for the most part they all mean essentially the same thing.

Within each responsibility center, the tasks may or may not be broken down into smaller units of responsibility, and so on until we reach the smallest possible unit of functional responsibility. Management's job is to plan the work of each unit, set the direction, organize all appropriate resources, and then control them. The impact of the organization is equal to the sum of all the individual functions controlled by the responsibility centers.

This style is suited to the nonprofits that the old national economy is likely to spawn: Large site-based programs for the mentally ill and mentally retarded, large hospitals, complex museums, sprawling universities. These types of nonprofits all require a major investment in property, plant, and equipment and the people and control systems to keep them running.

Throw out all of that conventional thinking for the future and start over again. In the industrialized economy, it was enough simply that these types of institutions existed. In the future, they will also need to perform. Government as a provider of direct services is in retreat. The commercial sector must strip down and compete in a global economy. What's left is a steadily increasing middle ground that must be tended by honest brokers, the time-honored role for nonprofits. But this time those brokers have got to produce in a different way, and to do so, they must reorient their financial systems from command and control to performance.

BEYOND MANAGEMENT CONTROLS IN THE 21ST CENTURY: HOW TO DO IT

As society demands greater emphasis on performance and as non-profits struggle to respond, there is a key fact which may or may not be reassuring, depending on one's perspective: *We are all making it up as we go along.* This is not a commentary on the competence of our overall performance but rather an acknowledgment of a sobering reality. We simply have not demanded that nonprofits organize for and deliver performance up to this point, so we are not all that good at it.

Plus, the landscape is shifting rapidly. Government at all levels must deal with shrinking resources and increasing demands on them, and the nonprofits that they work with are being forced to change accordingly. Starting in the 1980s, our health care system, one-seventh of the total Gross Domestic Product, entered into a gigantic experiment in reengineering, and no one yet has the slightest idea how it will all turn out. Higher education, it appears, will not be far behind. The one constant in these and other settings is that there will be a greatly increased demand for performance.

The obvious questions are: How do we do it? How do we organize for performance? How do we even define performance? What is the connection between the resources that go into a nonprofit and its performance? What is the proper role of the funder? The consumer? The manager? We will attempt to illustrate some real world answers to these questions by briefly describing three actual nonprofit entities and the performance orientations they devised. Then we will try to pull out of those stories the things that might provide guidance for the rest of us as we wrestle with similar problems in different settings.

Waukesha County Technical College

Waukesha County Technical College (WCTC) is one of 16 similar schools in Wisconsin. It offers associate degrees, vocational training, apprenticeship training, and adult education. For many years, the college has had a history of conducting various studies of institutional success, and in 1991 it carried out a longitudinal study of its 1986 graduates to learn how its former students' employment patterns had changed during the previous five years.

Two-thirds of the graduates responded to both surveys, which measured employment status, additional education or training since graduation, and the graduates' perceived importance of vocational/technical education. Surveyors asked about such factors as a graduate's employment status at the time of the survey, whether their employment was in a field related to their training, how much additional education graduates had received and in what, and whether graduates felt that their education at WCTC was important in getting a job and advancing in their careers.

Because the survey tracked the same group of students over time, college officials and faculty were able to get a dynamic picture of the changes and trends in one distinct subgroup of their market. More important, the survey provided feedback to faculty administration about course design, career counseling services, and other aspects of WCTC's mission. In addition, the board and the public at large were informed about the study's findings. After this study was completed, the president of the college announced that its board had adopted the goal that by the year 2000 a full 100 percent of its students would state that their experience at the school was "a wise investment of time and money."

The City of Portland, Maine

Some units of government are beginning to approach their services with a new zeal for measuring success. In 1993, the city of Portland, Maine, issued its third yearly report on city government performance, a document prepared by the office of the city auditor and her nine-person audit team. The report contains information on half a dozen of the city's major public services plus the results of a citizen survey and information from a handful of comparable cities around the country.

In many respects, the significant thing about this report is that it exists at all. In a time when governmental units' unresponsiveness has become a staple of stand-up comedians, headline stories, and old-fashioned complaining, the notion of a major city government publishing a report on its own performance is man-bites-dog news. In the report, the departments' performance was quantified according to performance indicators such as these from two sample departments:

Fire Services:

Lives lost to fires

Property loss from fires

Numbers of fires per 1,000 residents

Citizen satisfaction

Transportation Services:

Miles of unmet paving needs

Lane miles in good or very good condition

Citizen satisfaction

Some departments in the survey showed improvement, some stayed the same as the previous survey, and others got worse. It is safe to say, however, that the impact on the city came not from the results of any one department but from the simple act of public self-measurement.

Loomis House Nursing Home

Like many facilities of its kind, Loomis House, a nursing home in western Massachusetts, realized it had a communications problem. The evidence was all around, from residents' and families' gentle nudging to the staff's own experiences. A special cross-disciplinary team devised a number of solutions to various communications problems. We will recount two of them.

During mealtimes, nursing staff found themselves calling down to the kitchen for last-minute changes. Foods for use with medication would run out frequently, also necessitating a call. Either one of these situations resulted in delays in serving meals or certain medicines requiring food accompaniment, major flaws for any residential care facility. A careful analysis of several weeks' worth of specially designed telephone logs by the team revealed that most of the reasons for last minute changes and re-orders were quite preventable.

The solution was a modest redesign of certain procedures. Standing orders were replenished at night rather than first thing in the morning, thereby preventing delays. Food order sheets were slightly redesigned to accommodate additional choices. Most important, staff members who knew residents' food preferences best were brought into the food-ordering loop to give more personalized attention to the ordering process for each resident.

A second problem was that unmarked and therefore untraceable clothes kept appearing in the home's laundry. With 80 residents, it was not possible for anyone to have a visual inventory of everyone's clothing, so the unmarked pieces often went unreturned. This was a small, even annoying detail to staff but a major inconvenience and subtle sign of disrespect for residents.

Work on the solution occurred on two levels. First, one of the nurses suggested that a simple $4.95 laundry basket be clearly labeled "For Unmarked Clothes Only." This cut down on the incidence of unmarked clothes, but the big payoff was that in working through the solution, the multidisciplinary team realized that the real underlying issue was confusion about the standard admissions process that disguised itself as problems with the laundry, dietary, nursing communication, and so forth. The admissions process then became the next major focus for the team.

THE MORALS OF THE STORIES

There are some lessons here, and nonprofits of all kinds can move beyond simple management controls and toward a performance orientation if they learn them and act on them. The first is the fundamental importance of a clearly articulated mission. Having an understandable and widely accepted mission focuses an organization and makes decision making easier. It becomes an organizing principle as well as a foundation for measuring progress. How to set and maintain that mission is really not part of financial management, however, so we will not pursue the subject. For reference, see an earlier publication, *The Entrepreneurial Nonprofit Executive*.

The second point about these cases is that the nature of information gathering and processing must change in any organization the closer it moves to outcome-based management. Financial information typically takes up the greatest concentration of data processing resources in most nonprofits. In the future, it will have to share the power with outcome measures.

The City of Portland's example hints at the degree of effort that will be necessary to manage for performance in the future. The type of information used in their report may already exist in other cities, but if it does it is probably buried deep within each department. Some entity-wide office such as the auditor in Portland's case must tease the information out and maintain it in a consistent format in order for the measures to make sense over the years.

Performance-based nonprofit management will stress performance comparisons, known as benchmarks. The quantum leap that microprocessor technology took in the late 1980s and early 1990s—and the upcoming leaps to be made possible via the next generation of microchips—will make individualized benchmarking much easier. All that is needed now is the emergence of centralized authorities such as governments, trade associations, research groups, and private advisers to develop and disseminate benchmarks for use by their constituencies.

A third characteristic of a performance-oriented nonprofit is that its managers routinely and consistently ask consumers what performance means and how they are doing it. Surveys, it is safe to predict, are going to proliferate in future years until we figure out better and more efficient ways of soliciting formalized and statistically valid feedback from users. Both Portland and WCTC used highly formal and carefully designed survey tools. Loomis House did not, although it could have, because the smaller scope made it possible for consultants and staff to do the asking personally and because research on consumer preference was available for the industry. A more formalized program, however, would make use of written surveys.

The nonprofit committed to performance will also flatten itself. The traditional pyramid hierarchical style organization no longer works for most nonprofits. In its place is a flatter organization, made possible by improvements in communication technology and made necessary by the economic squeeze of the past decade or so. It no longer takes as long to get information from one level of the nonprofit to another, and this eliminates the need for at least part of the formerly intervening level of management at the middle of the pyramid. At the same time, executive levels will take a more direct role in managing internal performance standards, in part because funders will demand it and in part because there will be fewer managers to do it anyway.

Finally, the serious nonprofit manager will look for generally accepted performance standards and will eventually seek outside validation of its performance. Right now, few such independent verifiers exist. Accrediting and licensing bodies fill part of the void, but only a small part. Universities, research groups, and consultants are workable sources of performance verification at the moment, but in general there is a real lack of independent expertise available to conduct performance reviews. Note that Portland's own auditor conducted this study rather than an outsider. As funding sources increasingly ask for details on what was accomplished as opposed to the more traditional focus on what was spent, the traditional financial audit may recede in favor of a more outcome-oriented evaluation. It is even possible that an entirely new class of performance-verification entities will be invented to meet the demand for independent attestation of results, somewhat similar to the circulation confirmation services that newspapers and magazines currently employ.

HOW TO PREPARE—STRATEGIC BUSINESS SYSTEM POSITIONING

The single most important thing that any nonprofit executive, manager, or board member can do to prepare for the future world of performance measurement is what we call *strategic business system positioning*. In essence, this means that a nonprofit provides its administrative and financial systems the same type of strategic leadership as the agency as a whole frequently gets.

One of the problems with management control systems being rooted so firmly in financial and accounting records is that they become backward-looking activities. This way of thinking then permeates the whole administrative and financial function; programs and services run nimbly ahead while the administrative and financial systems are forced to play constant catch-up. To properly support the nonprofit of the twenty-first century, financial management must be closely linked to the overall mission, and must conceive of its role as designing and maintaining the information flow necessary to carry out that mission in a publicly accountable fashion. This orientation is different from today's single-minded focus on accountability, control, and responsibility. Board members, middle managers, and outside advocates will have to learn that accountability is only a precondition to performance, not an end in itself.

Strategic business system positioning amounts to systematizing the choices. (See Box.) The first element is simple and inexpensive. It is to think through ways to get the financial and administrative systems out in front of the information flow that will be necessary for the future. This requires in-depth familiarity with the organization's strategic direction and an understanding of what constitutes performance in the field. In areas as diverse as environmental services and health care, performance will increasingly be defined as prevention. That means that information systems, job descriptions, and printed output all need to be structured with that shift in mind.

The second and hardest element in strategic business system positioning is determining what information needs to be collected and how it should determine the output of "pure" accounting

---

Accountability Pressure Points and How to Change Them

Moving financial systems from control to performance involves recognizing the pressure points where change must occur. The details will vary with each organization, but here is a list of the way the orientations will change:

FROM	TO
External Demands for:	
"How did you spend the money?"	"What did you accomplish?"
Functions & programs	Consumer need
Services	Systems
Internal Approach Utilizes:	
Command	Influence
Control	Focus
Jobs	Roles
Responsibility	Empowerment
Individuals	Independent contractors

systems. This area is where the advances in information technology and the changing definitions of service are going to give individual nonprofits the opportunity to devise their own definitions, at least at first. But once a definition of performance settles in for a given field, all players will need to adopt it quickly.

Finally, business systems should be prepared to change quickly. From the beginning, there has been a static quality about nonprofit business systems, as though the goal was to attain a steady state of existence after years of fine tuning. If that were ever possible, it surely will not be attainable anytime in the future. Instead, systems must be decentralized as much as possible, with centralized oversight provided only for agency-wide services such as payroll and capital borrowing and for planning purposes such as a common chart of accounts and overall strategic direction.

In this new world of performance, every nonprofit "citizen" will feel an increased demand for financial literacy. The minimum standard for responsible participation in the affairs of a nonprofit will go up a notch or two. This is as it should be. The purpose of this whole chapter—and, indeed, of this entire book—is to provide you with some of the tools necessary for full participation in your own nonprofit organization. The linkage between the financial inputs of a nonprofit and its contribution to its society may at first seem indirect and abstract. This book can be considered a success if that link now seems a bit clearer and more direct.

APPENDIX

Using the Disk

DISK TABLE OF CONTENTS

Part III: Operations

Part IV: Control

INTRODUCTION

Streetsmart Financial Basics for Nonprofit Managers includes a diskette with a set of practical financial tools for overseeing the financial management of a nonprofit organization. Think of these files as a toolbox for *consumers* of financial information. For the most part, they are not the kind of computer files that bookkeepers and accountants typically use every day. Rather, they are designed for the nonfinancial specialist whose responsibility is to understand, analyze, and act upon the information that financial personnel produce.

Some of these files are drawn directly from exhibits contained in the book (e.g., financial analysis tools), while others attempt to put a general idea described in the book into a usable format (e.g., Economic Size Self-Test). Designed to be easily modified and adapted, the files are meant to save you time and to help produce insights that you would not normally get from routine financial information. Line items used in these forms usually correspond to the line items on the IRS Form 990, although different line items can easily be substituted.

The worksheets and reports are stored in two types of files:

- Spreadsheets are formatted for use with Lotus 1-2-3 Version 2.3 or higher. These files have the extension .WK1.
- Sample documents are provided in WordPerfect Version 5.1. These files have the extension .WP.

The files on this disk contain brackets—[ ]—to indicate information that you need to insert. Frequently, there is an identifying phrase within the brackets to describe the information needed. For example, [Organization] would indicate that you need to insert the name of your organization. Frequently, the brackets include on-screen commentary to give you instructions and tips for using them. Before saving and printing the files, make sure to replace all brackets with the appropriate inserts and to delete the bracketed on-screen instructions.

Forms used in any business context should be appropriate to their purpose and therefore must be carefully considered and adapted to each situation. Because no two situations are identical, modifying these forms will be necessary. Although the forms are generally believed to be reliable, they cannot be guaranteed to reflect the peculiarities and nuances of local practice. If accounting, legal, or other expert advice is required, the services of a competent professional should be sought.

COMPUTER REQUIREMENTS

The enclosed diskette requires an IBM PC or compatible computer with the following:

- IBM DOS or MS DOS 3.1 or later.
- A 3.5-inch disk drive.
- Lotus 1-2-3 Version 2.3 or higher.
- WordPerfect Version 5.1 or higher, or any word processor that can read WordPerfect files.

WYSIWYG on Lotus 1-2-3 or Lotus for Windows is highly recommended because spreadsheet files are easier to read and more visually pleasing when prepared with WYSIWYG or in Windows. Optional equipment includes a DOS compatible printer and a word processing package like Microsoft Word for Windows. If you have a different spreadsheet software package, consult your user manual for information on using Lotus files in your package. Most popular spreadsheet programs, including Microsoft Excel and Quattro, are capable of reading files formated for Lotus. Using the index in your software manual, refer to the section on "Converting Lotus Files" or on "Loading Files from Other Programs."

HOW TO MAKE A BACKUP DISKETTE

Before you use the enclosed diskette, we strongly recommend that you make a backup copy of the original. Making a backup copy of your disk allows you to have a clean set of files saved in case you accidentally change or delete a file. Remember, however, that a backup disk is for your own personal use only. Any other use of the backup disk violates copyright law. Please take the time now to make the backup copy, using the instructions below.

If your computer has two floppy disk drives:

1. Insert your DOS disk into drive A of your computer.
2. Insert a blank disk into drive B of your computer.
3. At the **A:>**, type **DISKCOPY A: B:** and press Enter. You will be prompted by DOS to place the source disk into drive A.
4. Place the first disk into drive A. Follow the directions on screen to complete the copy.
5. When you are through, remove the new backup disk from drive B and label it immediately. Remove the original disk from drive A and store it in a safe place.

If your computer has one floppy disk drive and a hard drive, you can copy the files from the enclosed disk directly onto your hard disk drive, in lieu of making a backup copy, by following the installation instructions.

INSTALLING THE DISKETTE

The enclosed disk contains 20 individual files in a compressed format. In order to use the files, you must run the installation program for the disk. You can install the diskette onto your computer by following these steps:

1. Insert the disk into drive A of your computer.
2. At the **A:>** type **INSTALL** and press Enter.
3. The installation program will be loaded. After the title screen appears, you will be given the options shown in Figure 1. The following Menu Selections will be listed: Edit Destination Paths, Select Destination Drive, Toggle Overwrite Mode, Select Groups to Install, and Start Installation.

```
McLaughlin/Financial Basics Installation Program

  Choose each of the following menu selections to configure
  the way in which McLaughlin/Financial Basics will be installed on your
  system.



        Edit destination paths   : \FNBASICS
        Select destination drive : C:
        Toggle overwrite mode    : Overwrite All
        Start installation



                        Item Description
        Allows you to edit each of the destination paths.



Press [ALT-X] to exit at any time
```

4. The **Destination Path** is the name of the default directory to store the data files. The default directory name is FNBA-SICS. To change this name, press Enter, hit the letter **P,** type in the name of the directory you wish to use, and press Enter again.
5. **Select Destination Drive** gives you the option of installing the disk onto a hard disk drive C:\ or, if you wish, onto a different drive.

6. The **Toggle Overwrite Mode** pertains to the directories you already have on your hard drive. Do *not* give the default directory the same name as an existing directory on your hard drive or the installation program will overwrite or delete any pre-existing directories of the same name.

The files are now successfully installed onto your hard drive.

USING THE FILES

Once you have installed the disk on your hard drive or made backup copies as instructed, you can begin to customize the files. The Lotus spreadsheets can be identified by the WK1 extension, and the WordPerfect documents can be identified by the WP extension. To use the spreadsheets and documents, load your software programs as usual. The files from this disk will be located in the subdirectory FNBASICS. For example, the file "Audit Equation Self-Test" can be found under C:\FNBASICS\EQUATION.WK1. When you are through using a file, you can save it under a new file name in order to keep the original file intact. For more information about using the spreadsheets and documents, consult the appropriate software user manuals.

DISK TABLE OF CONTENTS WITH COMMENTARY

File Name	Title
	Part I: Analysis
FINTASKS.WK1	**Key Financial Tasks of Nonprofit Organizations** Different types of nonprofit organizations present different types of financial management challenges. Use this chart to locate your type of nonprofit and pinpoint the corresponding financial pressure points.
MESSAGES.WK1	**Messages from the Balance Sheet** Educated readers can derive a great deal of information from a balance sheet. Here, in

summary form, is a guide to interpreting the messages your balance sheet is sending you, plus some suggestions for future action.

FINTOOLS.WK1   **Financial Statement Analysis Tools**
These financial analysis tools provide managers, board members, funders, regulators, and advocates with an invaluable portrait of an organization's fiscal health. All data needed to complete these financial analyses can be taken from a single year's IRS Form 990.

FINDEF.WP   **Financial Statement Analysis—Definitions**
This shorthand chart defines each of the tools used in the Financial Analysis Tools file.

FINFORM.WK1   **Financial Statement Analysis—Formulas for Ratios**
This file shows the actual formulas used in the Financial Analysis Tools file in a manner suitable for reprinting along side the analysis file itself.

ACTGUIDE.WK1   **Financial Action Guide for Nonprofit Organizations**
What happens once the financial analysis is complete? This file interprets what each tool may be telling you and suggests courses of action.

Part II: Accounting

MCOA.WK1   **A Model Chart of Accounts**
Bill Levis at Bernard M. Baruch College, City University of New York, has produced an innovative tool designed to help cross-walk a nonprofit's financial accounting system to the IRS Form 990. He was kind enough to let us include the Model Chart of Accounts for your use.

COSTALLO.WK1   **Cost Allocation Worksheet**
If you have ever wondered about the true cost of your nonprofit's services, use this form to learn the answers. For maximum benefit, keep the line items to a minimum and restructure the relationship between the "departments" as necessary.

EQUATION.WK1   **Audit Equation Self-Test**
Many nonprofit organizations do not understand what is expected of them as financial managers, and as a result they may produce poor financial audits. Use this file to evaluate your organization's degree of control over the audit process.

RFP.WP   **Sample Request for Proposal for Audit Services**
Whether it's time to seek a new auditor or simply to test the waters, use this file as a template for issuing a Request for Proposals. By leaving the structure of the response largely up to the bidders, this format allows the real flavor of each firm's style to come through.

Part III: Operations

CASHCHEK.WP   **Checklist for Cash Flow Projections**
Certain information is essential to have on hand when preparing a cash flow project. This time-saving checklist makes gathering the data an easier task.

CASHFLOW.WK1   **Cash Flow Projection Worksheet**
Ask your financial staff to complete this projection on a monthly or quarterly basis. Use the results to plan better use of your cash.

FRINGE.WK1   **Fringe Benefit Rate Calculation Worksheet**
Fringe benefits are good for employee morale, but they can be expensive. Use this worksheet to find out just how much they cost.

BUDGREP.WK1   **Sample Budget Format**
This file can help simplify the chore of budget development for a single program, an administrative and finance department, or an entire organization. It contains formulas designed to build in standard allocation percentages for such expenses as fringe benefits and indirect costs.

BUDGREP%.WK1   **Sample Budget Reporting Format—Percent Variance**
There are numerous ways to report revenues and expenses, and percent variances is one common method. The template can be modified to create just about any format desired.

BUDGREP$.WK1   **Sample Budget Reporting Format—Dollar Variance**
Dollar variance is another frequently used method.

BREAKEVN.WK1   **Project Break-Even Analysis**
To plan projects or ongoing budgets responsibly, managers need to know the projected break-even point. The break-even analysis file automatically calculates it once you enter complete data.

ECONSIZE.WK1   **Economic Size Self-Test**
The notion that there might be an economically efficient size for a nonprofit to provide certain types of services is just beginning to be understood. This file offers a way to test the influence of fixed costs, an important element of economic size, in a given nonprofit.

PROFPLAN.WK1 **Profit Planning Package**
Nonprofits need profit just as much as for-profit organizations need it (They just do something different with it). The Profit Planning Package translates the ideas about desired profit size in the text of this book into a single, easy-to-use spreadsheet.

Part IV: Control

CONTROLS.WK1 **Self-Evaluation of Internal Controls**
How effective is your system of internal controls? This handy matrix will spot potential weaknesses just by filling in the blanks with staff names. Draw a line from each name; wherever the lines cross, you have a potential weakness.

USER ASSISTANCE AND INFORMATION

John Wiley & Sons, Inc. is pleased to provide assistance to users of this package. Should you have any questions regarding the use of this disk, please call our technical support number, (212)850-6194, weekdays between 9 A.M. and 4 P.M. Eastern Standard Time.

To place additional orders or to request information about other Wiley products, please call (800)879-4539.

Index